TWO HAMPSHIRE FAMILIES
HANN / HISCOCK

PETER HANN

authorHOUSE®

AuthorHouse™
1663 Liberty Drive
Bloomington, IN 47403
www.authorhouse.com
Phone: 1-800-839-8640

Published by AuthorHouse   05/24/2012

ISBN: 978-1-4685-7924-6 (sc)
ISBN: 978-1-4685-7939-0 (e)

PREFACE

For a number of years I have wanted to record my knowledge, thoughts etc. of the two families from which I am born. I wanted to record my memories particularly of my grandparents and parents as they are people that I remember, but also I wanted to research a little further back so that I could understand a little more of their families and upbringing. My labour in writing may some day evolve into a book for all to read or may just be copied into some form of sheeted record to pass to my grandchildren.

I have on numerous occasions asked myself if the effort would be worth the trouble, but as years have gone by two events have shown me the way forward. Firstly to my surprise whilst looking through a bundle of papers left after my father had died I realized that he must have had a similar idea as laying in front of me was a collection of notes, information and thoughts that he had assembled during his last few years including details of the purchase of number 36 College Street, Petersfield by my grandfather and wartime travels in India and Burma.

Secondly, some years earlier I had met the late John Hayes a former English teacher at Petersfield School and spoke about my idea to which his immediate response was, "you must do it, we need to know about families past, their lives, their work, their troubles etc. You really must do it".

The underlying theme of my writing is to tell the story of two families from two different structures brought together by marriage. One is a hard working basic family suffering from the effects of a war and widowhood and often living on what would be termed today as well below the poverty line. The other family would be perhaps termed middle class with a little more income, but having still to work very hard, very hard to make ends meet. As poor as each one was the core parts of their lives were the family, their religous beliefs, their duty to their employer and their unwritten duty to their community.

The essence of each family has taught me much in my life and made me proud of my heritage. Socially there were differences particularly in the period just before the second world war when my parents first met, but in other ways they were so very similar.

FAMILY STRUCTURES

To understand any book about families it is essential to look at the family trees. For the Silver / Hiscock families I have only looked back to my greatgrandparents, but for the Hann / Bridge families I have been able to go a lot further back in time for the Hann side thanks to records given to me many years ago by my great aunt May who lived to see her second century in Bournemouth. To avoid confusion I have kept to recording the history detail from my grandparents on both sides, but have added some notes at the end which may be of assistance to anyone wishing to investigate further.

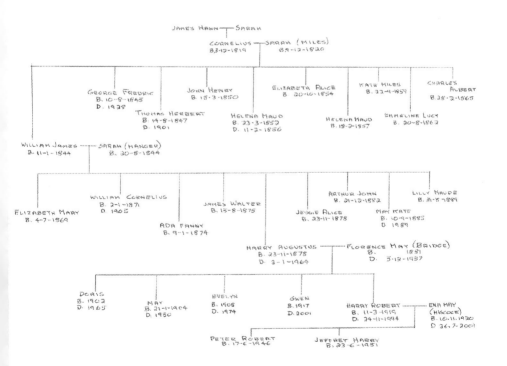

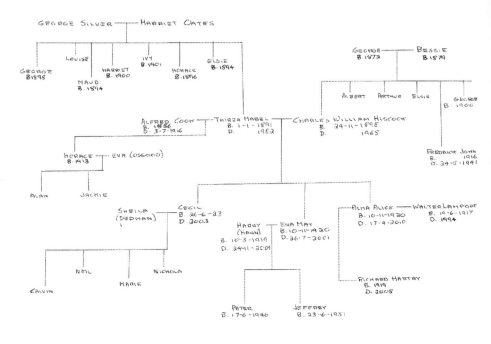
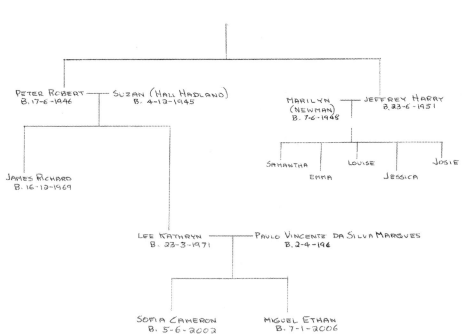

THE SILVER FAMILY

I always understood that my grandmother was born Thurza Mabel Silver, but investigation into the now freely available records shows her name to be Thurza Mable Oates. Cross checking this with the remainder of the family names in the records shows that in 1901 aged 10 she lived with her mother Harriet, father William and brothers and sisters Elsie 8, George 3, Gertrude 5 months, Harriet 1, Horace 5 and Maud 7 in Hampshire having been born in Basing, Hampshire. Investigation into Thirza`s early life has been difficult, but the assumption is that her mother Harriet was unmarried at the time of her birth in 1891, but in 1892 had married William Silver as the records show that when the next child, Elsie was born in about 1894 Harriet and William are recorded as being mother and father. Until about 1906 the family home appears to have been Long Sutton near Odiham, Hampshire, but by 1912 the home was Boulinge Hill Farm Buriton where William was a farm foreman.

In addition Thirza`s surname documents show her both as Thirza Mabel and also Mabel Thirza. Not easy for the investigator to find information regarding her birth and early years. Maybe by the time this book is completed I will have answered the question.

There is no evidence to suggest that William was not Thirza`s father. Although in a different time with different values the marriage may just not have taken place until after the arrival of Thirza. Alternatively the father may be someone unknown who, for his own reasons, could not marry Harriet. William`s home appears to have been Long Sutton whereas Harriet came from Herriard just about three miles away.

When I was a child grandma and I often spoke about her family, but this subject never arose so we may never know where her real foundation was. Of her siblings I well remember Elsie, Harriet and Horace as a child in Petersfield. George died in the First World War, Maud and Louis I can only just remember meeting and Ivy was the late arrival who I remember well. I think Gertrude was in fact Louis. The elder children are all shown on records as having been born at Long Sutton.

The 1901 Census Records show that Thirza lived at Long Sutton, Odiham and also at Ashe Warren, Oakley, Basingstoke in 1907 and Broad View, Petersfield in 1909. The latter would have been domestic / housekeeping jobs. The 1911 Census Records show that Thirza was a parlour maid with the Gammon family in Petersfield. Mrs Gammon at 55 was a widow with a son of 17 and a daughter, Hilda who was 12. Also in the household was a cook aged 29 whose name we only know as Lilly.

Thirza was married at the age of 20 to Alfred George Cook at Buriton near Petersfield in 1911. Alfred was baptised at Buriton in 1886 so was 25 when he married.

By 1914 Alfred was a farm labourer for P & S Seward at Weston and they moved to Weston by 1915. In 1913 Thirza gave birth to their son Horace who was shown to be attending Buriton school from 1919 to 1927.

The idyllic countryside beneath the downs would be cherished by the 2012 population as a place away from the hustle and bustle of the twenty first century life, but the days were hard and the income very low in agriculture. The world was to change however with dramatic lifechanging results.

The call to arms in 1914 / 1915 resulted in Alfred enlisting in the 1st Btn. The Hampshire Regiment. As with many men at that time their consciences were singular and he told Thirza only after the enlistment was completed. It was very clear then and even from our conversations in my younger days that Thirza loved Alfred very much and for him to have enlisted without telling her first hurt her very much.

By the end of June 1916 Alfred found himself in the Somme Valley in Northern France in the area of Beaumont Hamel. The following day, July 1st he woke early and joined his comrades at the Front for that famous battle. This was to be his last battle as along with so many others on that day he suffered serious injuries. He was taken to the 4th Casualty Clearing

Station at Beauval, but died of his wounds on 3rd July. He is buried at the Beauval Communal Cemetary (Grave Reference F3). The gravestone shows his age as 34 whereas he was 30. The Hants & Sussex newspaper of 26th July 1916 published the following obituary: "Another soldier, well known and respected at Weston and Buriton, has, we regret to state, died as a result of his wounds received in France on July 1st. This was Pte. A.G.Cook, of the 1st Hampshire Regt., who was a native of Buriton. He was 30 years of age, married, and leaves a widow and a child. Prior to his enlistment about a year ago he was employed by Messrs. P and C Seward of Weston, where his widow, for whom much sympathy is felt, resides".

After Thirza and Horace's sad, but proud goodbye when he left for France, the shock and sadness on hearing of his death must have been unbearable. The love of Thirza's life had gone. Alfred had given his life for Thirza and Horace and for his country in what would turn out to be one of the bloodiest battles of the First World War. Devastated and numbed she would have to build a new life centred around Horace. The love of her life had gone, but was never forgotten. To the end of her life Alfred was in her heart and a much treasured portrait photograph in his soldiers uniform remained in a prominent location wherever she lived. Sadly this photograph was lost when she died, but others remain and are recorded here.

From the earliest part of my life in Rushes Road, Petersfield I had known Ken, Peter and John Marshall and remember well their mother and father. They had always been considered as good friends and were well known in the Petersfield of the 1950's and 1960's. It was at my fathers funeral in 1994 whilst in conversation with Peter he said "of course we are sort of related really". Asking how this could be he told me that Alfred Cook was his mother's brother. The conversation continued with Peter telling me that he had carried out some research into the short life of his uncle and his death in France. All information obtained about Albert Cook has either been given by Peter Marshall or stems from that information from official records. Forever grateful Peter.

After the First World War there were many widows with offspring such as Thirza and life must have been very hard. She remained in Weston and must have suffered poverty unknown in the twenty first century. It is most likely that she took domestic work to make ends meet with the family giving help to look after Horace. In my lifetime she had more than one cleaning job at any one time so this may well have been the case from 1916. To add to the grief Thirza`s brother George had also been killed during the war. Gunner 19905, "C" Battery, 70th Brigade Royal Field Artillery, George was seven years younger than Thirza and was killed in action on the 2nd July 1917 almost a year to the day Albert Cook had died. He is buried in Brandhoek Military Cemetary, Ieper, West-Vlaanderen, Belgium.

Private Alfred Cook with his wife Thirza and son Horace taken just
before Alfred left for France around 1915 / 1916

The widowed Thirza with Horace. This type of photograph was taken in many families after the loss of a husband and father during the First World War as was the last photograph of Alfred, Thirza and Horace. At this time Thirza was about twenty four years old.

A later photograph of Thirza and Horace with Horace looking every part the man of the house and Thirza looking a little happier since the first "widow" photograph

THE HISCOCK FAMILY

Charles (Charlie) William Hiscock was born in Petersfield in 1898 the first borne child of Bessie and George Hiscock. Records show that George and Bessie lived in East Meon near Petersfield, George being an above ground quarryman. It is most likely that at the time of Charlie's birth the family had moved to Retreat, Stroud. Two years after Charlie's arrival Bessie gave birth to a second son George. In later years the family grew with the arrivals of Elsie, Arthur, Albert and Fredrick (John).

Elsie married Jim Berriman, Arthur also married whilst Albert and Fredrick were unmarried. The family home in Petersfield is unknown although it could have been at Tilmore Farm, Bell Hill Ridge off the road from Petersfield to Steep where George junior lived during the 1950's / 1960's. Elsie and Jim lived in a cottage at Rothercombe Farm, Stroud during the 1950's and had one son, Michael who unfortunately died before his parents leaving a wife Jean and several daughters. Albert died suddenly in the 1960's whilst the dates of George's and Arthur's passing are unknown.

Like his brother Arthur, Fredrick was a Royal Marine. He had grown up being known by his second name John. At the early part of the Second World War he joined the battleship HMS Hood as part of the small number of Royal Marines always forming part of a battleships crew. In 1941 he returned home on shore leave, but felt uneasy about returning to the ship. So much so that he said that he would not go back at the end of his leave and his brother Charlie had to see him to the Dockyard gates to ensure that he rejoined the Hood. Little did anyone know that his fears were founded and this would be the last time the family would see John. On 24th May 1941 the Mighty Hood engaged the German battleship Bismarck in the Denmark Strait between Greenland and Iceland. A direct hit to the Hood blew it apart and 1418 members of the crew perished including 25 year old John. The family were devastated and in particular his nieces Ena and Alma and nephew Cecil The twins were only five years younger than John and therefore more like cousins than nieces. The very popular John had gone from them in a violent war. As with Thirza and her two losses in the First World War the whole family forever mourned his loss. Although I was born after John's death my mother spoke often of him such that I am able to record these details in later years.

Whilst searching the web for details of HMS Hood I became aware of the HMS Hood Association and its links with The Hood Chapel in St John The Baptist Church at Boldre in The New Forest. Scanning the records of the fateful crew of the ship I came across the name of Marine Fredrick John Hiscock. Whilst the details were correct there was no photograph of him. Remembering the photographs belonging to my aunt Alma I realised that I could rectify the omission and after obtaining agreement from Alma I submitted scanned copies of two portrait photos of John in Royal Marine uniform to the Association. These are now noted on the website and a proud feeling of family duty to my great uncle exists. Forevermore the fallen Marine can be remembered.

Details of how Thirza and Charlie first met are unknown, but during the First World War he was a Military Policeman, 7681614, and rose to the rank of Lance Corporal. The two came together possibly around 1918, but this is not confirmed. The first records known are 1920 when Alma and Ena were born.

The first family home was in Weston where Charlie possibly moved into Thirza and Horace's home. By July 1941 the move had been made to 25 Tilmore Road, Petersfield which is where I first encountered my grandparents.

Marine Frederick John Hiscock. This photograph has also been given to the HMS Hood Association and is shown on their website memorial. The "Mighty Hood" is shown in all her glory as a battleship

MY GRANDPARENTS, HISCOCK

The family that arrived at 25 Tilmore Road, Petersfield comprised Horace who was Thirza`s eldest son (whose father was Alfred Cook), the twins, born on November 10th 1920 and Thirza`s second son Cecil born on 26th June 1923.

All the children spent their childhood days in Weston and attended Buriton Junior School before moving on to Petersfield Secondary School. All children would have been confirmed at St Mary`s Church in Buriton. I can remember my father saying that when he first met my mother she lived at Weston so the move to Petersfield would have been just before the Second World War.

Life would have been quite difficult for any family living in an agricultural environment in the 1920`s, but Thirza always ensured that the family were well fed, dressed and looked after to the best of her ability. The movement of families away from their homes was relatively unusual at that time so the children would often have been in contact with aunts, uncles and cousins as well as their grandparents. One cousin who spent a considerable time with the family was Roy Silver who was about four years older than the twins.

The children developed their characters as they grew. Ena had dark hair, was rather quiet and at times very serious about life. Alma was blonde and very much enjoyed life whereas Cecil could be described as "a holy terror", "scamp", "pickle" or at times a title of far stronger words. His childhood aim was to antagonize his stepbrother, older sisters and parents as much as possible in which he succeeded. He would try his utmost to avoid doing any chore set for him and had felt his father`s belt on many an occasion for his errors. One such time occurred when the family had moved into Petersfield. Cecil had decided to climb onto the statue of King William III in the Square and despite demands from the local Constabulary would not come down. His father was duly Summoned to The Square and Cecil was eventually removed from the horse to feel the belt again.

The hamlet of Weston consisted only of a few houses and a farm. Weston Farm was well known for the growing of hops up until the 1950's. From the time of Alfred Cook's employment until after the Second World War the ownership of the farm was held by the Seward family, but at some time later the incombents were the Winser family. As in any farming community the most important time of the year was harvest time. Whether permanently employed or not you were expected to join others gathering the harvest and Thirza would be one of that number. I remember her often using the phrase "to earn a few shillins". Those few "shillins" were so important to her and the family in the 1920's / 1930's

Many hours would have been spent harvesting the hops and all the children would be involved. The three eldest would be of some help, but to Cecil it would be a big game. To be truthful he would be of little use to the harvest effort.

The hop harvest has been captured for all to see by the Petersfield artist Flora Twort. Her painting of the harvest from 1935 illustrates the toil and shows two young girls watching the work being carried out. One of the girls has very dark hair. Could this be Ena? Whether it is or not it represents so clearly stories told to me by my mother about the harvest as well as the life in the English countryside at that time such that a print of Flora's painting hangs in our lounge.

Digressing, to see the Petersfield area before the Second World War recorded on canvas a visit to The Flora Twort Gallery in Petersfield is highly recommended. I can remember seeing Flora in the town as a child. Little did I realise then how much she did to record life in Petersfield for all to see.

As with all families the time comes for the children to "flee the nest". Horace married Eva Osgood and lived for many years in Station Road next to Urquarts Garage. They had two children, Alan and Jackie. Horace, Eva and Alan died some years ago, but Jackie died in September 2011.

Cecil left school and within a year just before the second world war. Sometime after the commencement of the war he was called up for military service. Most of his working life was spent in the transport industry primarily in road haulage, but with a considerable amount of time in coach driving. His knowledge of the roads of Britain was extensive and he became a highly respected man after his early years of mischief. When away from the driving wheel he played football and eventually became an FA referee in the Portsmouth area. Cecil remained single until he was 30 and then married Sheila Dedman of Cowplain. His children Calvin, Marie, Neil and Nicola all live in the Catherington, Denmead, Cowplain and Portsmouth area. Sadly Cecil passed away in 2003 after a long battle with ill health although Sheila remains in Denmead.

My lasting memories of Cecil will always be the "chatting times" that we had in his later years at Horndean. All subjects would be covered, but particularly transport and some notable areas of the country which we had found on our travels. Whilst I am not a particular follower of sport the subject would always be covered with interest.

Alma married Walter (Wally) Lamport of Ash, Surrey in July 1941. Wally was a career soldier in The Royal Artillery and was later to experience the Dunkirk evacuation and the Burma Campaign.

Alma moved to Ash after her marriage and lived with Wally's parents and younger siblings. For eighteen years she worked as a bus conductress with the Aldershot & District Traction Company before health matters dictated that she take a somewhat warmer office job. Wally later also joined "The Tracco" as a driver where he remained until retirement. Sadly he passed away in 1994. In 1995 Alma married a former collegue Ted Hartry and moved to Ted's home at Reading Road in Farnborough later moving to a ground floor flat at Arnella Court in Queens Road, Farnborough. Ted developed Dementia and after a period in hospital and in care moved to Manor Place Nursing Home in Church Lane East in Aldershot where he remained until his death in 2008. Alma had joined Ted in Manor Place and remained there until her death on 17th April 2010.

By the time the family had moved to Petersfield Charlie had left the Military Police and was working for the GPO Telephones. The details of how he started this work and how he initially progressed are unclear, but by the late 1940's he was in charge of one of the two Morris Commercial line installation trucks with Horace as his driver. The second Petersfield based truck which was identical was the charge of Charlie's brother George. Charlie's vehicle was registered GYY 41 whereas Georges was GYY 31 both from about 1944 / 1946 vintage. Comparitively easy to identify by a young boy looking out for his grandad.

Charlie remained with the GPO until retirement. He had been a member of the Petersfield Home Guard from the Second World War until its demise. I can remember him telling me about exercises still being carried out long after the war had finished. For a short time after retirement he was a caretaker at the Petersfield High School Annex in College Street and also worked at the army stores unit at Liphook. Sadly his retirement was not long and he succumbed to cancer dying in 1964.

A small sideline carried on by Charlie was to cut up old unuseable pine telegraph poles into wood for lighting the coal fuelled open house fires. The method of lighting a fire was to ignite small lengths of wood and newspaper and to add small amounts of coal to ensure ignition to which would be added larger amounts of coal once the fire was fully alight. The small pieces of wood known as pimpwood were an essential part of the process in all but the wealthiest of households. The large shed at the bottom of the garden at number 25 always had an odour of pitched pine about it and the floor consisted of compressed wood shavings.

As a boy I would often call in to see my grandparents at Tilmore Road. There was always something to eat and drink and I particularly used to like to look into the front room. This was an area devoted to the past. An excellent example of a Victorian room with a large plant in a pot on a wooden stand, an abundance of china and glass, chairs that were deemed too good to sit on and the ever present portrait picture of Alfred Cook in his army uniform. In addition there remained a second world war gas mask, a military helmet and grandma's ARP helmet from her fire watching duties in Kimbers Field opposite No 25. Everything that a young boy would want to play with.

Sadly when my father took on the task of clearing the house in later years when grandma moved to Weston House he disposed of the contents of the room to the local authority dump. Who knows what more we could have learnt about the family had the important items been retained?

Still in my possession is one of the first world war brass shell cases which was opened out with the removal of all dangerous items and became a flower vase. My mother became the owner after grandma died and I have assumed the ownership after my parents died.

I cannot ever remember my grandmother not doing something. She carried out house cleaning duties for a number of people in Petersfield and had many friends as well as her brother and sisters in the town. All had to be kept in contact with or at least conversed with should she meet one of them in the town. She would come to our house once a week, usually a Thursday afternoon, and have a cup of tea. There was always something for her to tell us about someone or something.

Her domestic work over the years had taken a toll on her hands. Arthritis was severe in her fingers, every joint enlarged and deformed. Damp or wet days gave her considerable pain, but still she smiled at us.

Grandma's last years at Tilmore Road were still not wealthy times. No fitted carpets or strong decoration as we may expect in the twenty first century. Lino covered the floors downstairs with the occasional rug in the living room. Bare boards were the bedroom floors again with single rugs adjacent to the beds. The kitchen floor consisted of tiles which showed signs of wear in the doorways and by the sink. All hot water had to be boiled on the cooker as the earthenware sink only had a brass cold tap. Finally the antiquated outside toilet had an overall wooden seat with a high level cast iron cistern. This was a place that you visited out of necessity and left as soon as you could afterwards. Although a small paraffin lamp was kept on in the winter this was to me the coldest place on earth.

The occasional long term visitor took lodgings with Thirza and Charlie over the years at Tilmore after Ena and Alma married. I have spoken about Roy Silver, Thirza's nephew, who was disabled. A friendly character who went on to operate his own taxi service in Petersfield. There was also a man called Terry.

In the 1950`s / 1960`s holidays as we know it had not developed into the "must get away to the sun" craze. The furthest Thirza and Charlie travelled was usually to Alma and Wally at Aldershot. Whether a long weekend or a full week this would be the change of scenery for them.

As a young boy of about eight I remember grandma taking me to visit a relative in Midhurst. We travelled on the now closed Petersfield to Midhurst railway line which was my only journey on the route as it closed in 1955. Being even then very interested in transport I well remember the day and the journey back on a Southdown Motor Services pre war Leyland Titan double decker. These things stay in my mind. Unfortunately I cannot remember much about the lady we visited.

Cancer is a disease which when deep routed has but one message. The time on this earth is limited. Advances in medical science has meant near normal life spans for many people today and the easement of pain for those whose disease cannot be cured.

For Charlie the cancer was at an advance stage and incurable. This was to be a teenager`s first experience of a close family member dying from this disease. I remember seeing him laying in his bed without strength and hardly able to speak to me just a few days before he died in 1965. Normally tall and with a friendly character he was now an image that I did not want to remember him as.

I have few photographs of Grandad, but I am proud to have in my safe possession his military police batton complete with its decorated silver tips.

Although Thirza stayed at Tilmore Road for a short time after Charlies death she was eventually lucky to be allotted a ground floor flat in Weston House, Borough Road, Petersfield recently built by Petersfield Urban Distict Council. These were the first warden assisted flats for elderly people to be built in the area and consisted of centrally heated single or double units with a common room and laundry room.

Moving to Weston House gave some new strength to her and she enjoyed not only the time with new neighbours, but she was also able to walk to the town and to our house (now at College Street) talking to a few friends and acquaintances on the way. She was able to attend some of the Sunday morning services at the Salvation Army Hall in Swan Street.

The long rented house at 25 Tilmore Road was sold by its owners. When H A Hann & Son were asked to carry out modernization works to the property by the new owners it seemed strange to be demolishing the old kitchen and outside facilities to bring the house up to the twentieth century.

At 89 Thirza suffered a stroke which gave some paralysis to one side of her body. She was unable to take care of herself and was admitted to the Heathside Hospital in Durford Road, Petersfield. Realising that her time was limited the family and hospital staff celebrated her 90th birthday with tea and cake. A special visitor was our golden retriever Beth who had become a firm favourite with Thirza. At Weston there were dogs in the family and she just felt at home with the animal.

Other patients at Heathside enjoyed Beth's visit. A therapy that has now been recognised by medical people. Beth also enjoyed the visit as there was an abundance of food offered to her.

In 1982 Grandma passed away at the age of 91.

The top photographs show Ena, Alma and Cecil in schooldays at Buriton School whilst the lower photograph also includes Horace and is probably taken at Weston in the garden. The lower photograph of Cecil gives the impression that he has mischief on his mind.

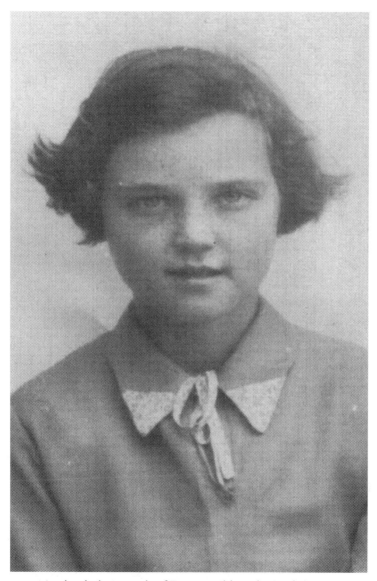

A school photograph of Ena, possibly in her early teens.

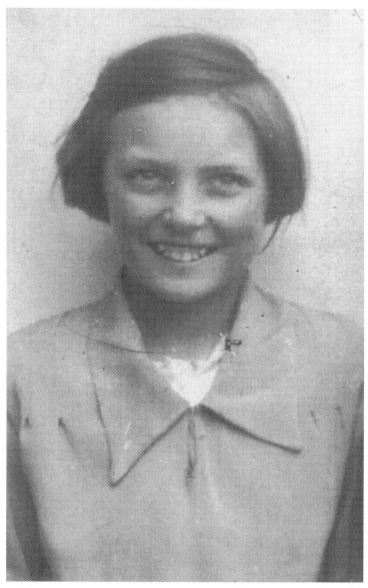

A school photograph of Alma taken at the same time as that of
Ena in the 1930s

Alma in the 1940`s. Alma`s husband, Wally Lamport standing with Arthur
Hiscock and Alma and Wally`s wedding photograph of August 1941.
Thirza and Charlie can be seen as well as Margo and Jean Chitty
on the left and centre of the photograph

A wedding day photograph of Cecil Hiscock
with his new wife Sheila (Dedman).

Grandad Charlie Hiscock pictured at 25 Tilmore Road, Petersfield.

Few photographs of Charlie remain, but this one shows him in
his later years relaxing.

THE BRIDGE FAMILY

Florence May Bridge was born at Prittlewell, Southend-on sea, Essex in 1881. She was the second child and first daughter of George and Esther Bridge. Both George and Esther came from Essex and George was a brickmaker. Florences eldest brother was Arthur born in 1877 followed by Florence and then Walter (1883), Mabel (1887) and Sidney (1889).

The family were very much Essex people. George was born in North Benfleet in 1851 and Esther (Scraggs) was born in Prittlewell in 1854. Esther's family came from a line of Keys and Trufs by name and had associations with Purleigh in Essex. George's parents were William, born in Little Stanbridge in 1829 and Eliza (Aven) born in Runwell.

By 1881 the family home was at East Street, Prittlewell and this was to remain so until Mabel died. The children would have gone to local schools. Information regarding Arthur does not exist, but it is assumed that at least his image is recorded in one of the many family photographs in my possession. Walter married and lived locally, but his profession is unknown. I remember them visiting Petersfield when I was young and at least two visits I made with one or both of my parents to their home on the outskirts of Southend. There is no knowledge of any offspring.

Mabel married Will Jeffries who at some time was a tram driver in Southend. I remember Uncle Will as a very tall man although from a child's point of view everyone is tall. However, Mabel was very short which probably exaggerated the memory. Holidays were often spent at Petersfield and I can remember waiting with my grandfather at the workshop door in College Street for the Westcliffe-on-sea & District coach to set them down across the road. Mabel and Will had one son Bert who became an estate agent in Southend living to over ninety years. After marriage to Kathleen they had two daughters Jennifer and Susan.

The memories of Walter and his wife together with Mabel and Will are of friendly and kind people although the last time I saw any of them would have been no later than 1963.

The youngest member of the family whom I never met was Sidney who had emigrated to New Zealand. In his youth he was a lover of the music halls in Southend and enjoyed having a good time. Whilst visiting the establishments he befriended a young Salvation Army girl who had clearly taken his heart. His enthusiasm was dampened a little when she told him that she was soon to emigrate to New Zealand with her family. Not to be put off by this Sidney told her that he would go with her, marry her in New Zealand and then bring her back to England. He went to the new country with his love, married her, but stayed in New Zealand joining the Salvation Army and rising to the third in seniority in the country. The couple had four children, two boys and two girls and during their lives were very highly regarded for not only their religious commitment and work, but also their humanitarian work.

Of their family, in 2012 one daughter in her nineties, Joyce, remains as does son Ken in his late eighties. During 2008 I made contact with Sidney's second daughter Gwen and also Andy, whose grandfather was the first son Selwyn, whom I had met in Petersfield when I was in my late teens. Sadly on November 18th 2010 Gwen died at the age of 94. We had spoken on the telephone and written to each other about our lives, families etc. Gwen had sent me a copy of her book telling her life story from being a Salvation Army officer's "kid" to her adult years and her life in New Zealand. The link remains and armed with a New Zealand family tree a visit to the family is planned for a future date.

THE HANN FAMILY

Harry Augustus Hann was born on 23rd November 1878 in one of the houses overlooking the seafront promenade at Weymouth in Dorset. His twin sister Alice Jesse brought William and Sarah Hann`s offspring to an eventual nine.

Harry`s father and mother had moved to Weymouth from Yeovil by 1866 where to this day the Hann name is well known. The family tree shows that in the early part of the nineteenth century the family home was in Beaminster, Dorset.

By 1881 the family had moved to the still quiet small town of Bournemouth where William continued his profession an an Undertaker, W.J.Hann. His company remained in existence until at least the 1970`s being in later years controlled by the Morgan offspring of the family.

My grandfather who I always called "Pop" told me many stories of his childhood in Bournemouth. By all accounts he was a bundle of trouble and always fighting (as children do) with his twin sister. Many a time his father would make him sit in a new coffin while he polished it. It may have been that the family home was at Westbourne, Bournemouth initially, but by the time of the following event the family had moved to St Swithens Road.

The family at this time were staunch Baptists and attended the Landsdown Baptist Church in Bournemouth regularly. The children were members of the Sunday School which in those days would most likely involve a pre morning service session plus an hours session on Sunday afternoon. Attendance records were usually made by stamping an ink star onto a card issued annually to each scholar. Prizes could be won for the highest number of stars obtained in the year.

There came on the scene one Harry Hann. He would go to Sunday School as decreed by his parents entering through the front door of the school hall, have his card stamped and promptly escape through the window of the toilet and off down the street to meet up with his friends. He didn`t seem to have been missed so all was well until on one Sunday at teatime his father asked him what the story was about at Sunday School that afternoon. He tried to wriggle his way out of the difficult question by saying that he could not remember. His father severely chastised him for missing the lesson as he had taken an afternoon walk and had seen his errant son playing with his friends in the town.

At sometime around 1971 I was the mechanical contractor`s engineer for the then new Town Hall extension in Bournemouth. A colleague of mine held a similar position with the same company for an office block refurbishment in Oxford Road, Bournemouth. Whilst awaiting him on site at Oxford Road I casually looked across the road and realised I was looking at the Baptist Church that my grandfather used to attend. My eyes went to a small window with reeded glass at the end of a path to the right of the main church. Was I looking at the window that was the means of grandfathers escape? I remember smiling to myself.

On leaving School at about twelve years old Harry became a plumbing apprentice with local ironmonger Bacon & Curtis. During his time with Bacon & Curtis he developed an excellent craft skill which was to be his provider of income for the rest of his life. Apart from working in some of the hotels and large houses being built in Bournemouth he also carried out plumbing repairs and installation in the Westbourne Hospital, Poole Road.

One undisputed story he would tell was of a day when he and some of his workmates were instructed to go to the Bournemouth West Railway Station, await a train from Yeovil and collect a car being sent from the Peerless factory in the Somerset town. Once received they were instructed to push the car to the town centre ready for its display in a carnival a few days later. As many will be aware the town of Bournemouth is very hilly in places and temptation overtook the task force when they climbed aboard and rode down the hill to The Square. My father questioned the truth of this story one day when an old friend of Harry`s from his days at Bacon &

Curtis visited us at College Street. Without doubt it was true. It was about 1890 and Harry had ridden on one of the first if not the first car to run in Bournemouth. Times have changed.

Another story from Harrys early days concerned the reason why he always walked with one foot turning inwards. We were told that he had come to the rescue of a lady and child who were riding in a small horse drawn trap when the horse was startled and bolted. He ran to help and was kicked by the horse as he stopped it so saving the lady and child from injury or worse. This action would not be the first time in Harrys life that he would be quick to come to someones aid without thought for himself.

The beach at Bournemouth would have been considerably quieter around 1890, most people enjoying the expanse of sand being from the locality or would have travelled to the town by rail via the main line from London and Southampton, the line from Salisbury or the line from the Midlands which ran down to the coast from Bath across The Mendips to Templecombe and the Dorset countryside. One visitor to Bournemouth in 1898 to visit her sister was Florence Bridge from Southend.

Florence had decided to take in the beach one day and by chance met with a young Harry. Doubts are always cast at holiday romances, but this one lead to a fifty seven year marriage for Harry and Florence for in 1900 they were married at St Mary`s Church, Prittlewell, Southend.

Of Harry`s family, Elizabeth married to become Elizabeth Bath living at Sutton, Surrey, William Cornelius died in 1905, Ada married to become Ada Rogers and remained in Bournemouth, James died early in life, Harry`s twin Jessie married and became Jessie Leydell emigrating to South Africa, Arthur married Hilda and moved to Salisbury as a hairdresser, May remained a spinster living to 104 in Bournemouth and Lilly married and became Lilly Niblet moving to Bristol. I remember meeting Ada, May, Lilly and Arthur in my younger years.

My great grandfather William James Hann the father of Harry snr.

MY GRANDPARENTS, HANN

The first home recorded for Harry and Florence was Florence Villas, Clarence Road, Sudbury, Suffolk where Doris was born on 20th August 1902 and May on 21st January 1904 respectively. However, recently provided information suggests that by 1900 Harry had left Bournemouth and was living in Rochford, Essex. This ties in with the fact that Harry and Florence were married in 1900 and therefore it could be assumed that their first home together was in fact in Rochford. His employment at this time was with H Wyeth at 94 Park Road, Southend.

In March 1900 Harry left Wyeth and went to work for Victoria Engineering Co in Sudbury as a gas fitter where he remained until 1904.

At the time of May`s birth on 21st January 1904 Harry`s twin sister Alice was living with them at Florence Villas. This may have been solely to give help to Florence with a young baby plus a two year old. As Harry and Florence`s relationship in later years with Alice was somewhat strained little was said about his twin sister by my Grandfather in his last years. Alice emigrated to South Africa living in Cape Town.

In August 1904 Harry and Florence moved to Hungerford in Berkshire where Harry was employed by the local ironmonger G J Hawkes. It was in 1908 that Evelyn was born.

Mr Hawkes considered Harry to be "thoroughly honest, sober, trustworthy and a very good workman" and very much regretted losing him when Florence`s health required a move to another area. A recommendation letter to a future employer written on 26th May 1909 survives.

The next home was at Cobham in Surrey where Harry was employed by another ironmonger, a Mr Allsworth. At some time Harry was asked if he would move with Mr Allsworth to open a new shop in Lavant Street,

Petersfield after the takeover of Lewis the ironmonger and in 1912 the family had moved to Petersfield living in Charles Street initially before moving to 34 College Street.

With three young children aged 10, 8 and 5 Harry would have had to work hard to keep everyone fed and clothed so when Mr Allsworth refused to increase his wages from 6 old pence an hour to 10 old pence an hour some serious decisions had to be made. A shed was erected in the garden and in 1913 the firm of H A Hann commenced operations. The local Urban District Council came to hear of this shed being erected and demanded that it should be demolished. Harry ignored them and got on with his work.

In 1917 Florence gave birth to her fourth daughter, Gwen. Poor Harry really wanted a son, but it did seem that this wasn`t going to happen. Eventually on 11th March 1919 his wish was granted when Florence presented him with a son, Harry junior. The shout "it`s a boy" went up and for most of his life Harry junior`s family nickname was "Boy".

The family was now complete and Petersfield had become very much the family home. A major happening however had yet to take place which would change the life of the family. This would not be an overnight change, but a significant change and one which would provide the family "shrine" for the Hann family then, their children and their grandchildren.

Whilst looking through the notes my father left I found his writings of the events leading to the move to 36 College Street. These are repeated as follows:

"The late H A Hann acquired No 36 College Street in 1919 for £600-00 Freehold from The South Eastern Farmers Limited. A family by the name of Marshall rented the property from the owners and a period of four years passed before they could be removed. When the Hann family eventually moved in Mrs Hann opened the shop which formed part of the property as a sweet shop.

Behind the shop there was a brick built bake house with a brick oven where bread etc was baked. At the end of the bake house there was a well of some fourty foot depth. In later years Harry demolished the bake house and filled in the well with brick rubble.

Inside the house, partly over the kitchen and in the centre of the building was a funnel like structure about ten feet square. It had iron bars across the top to form a grating where barley was allowed to dry. It was understood that some form of heat was placed under to form a drier.

A neighbour who has long since passed on told me that she would go to a half doorway in the building with her jug to buy home brewed beer. This was before the single storey front shop was built. In the outer wall were recesses with half iron baskets fixed to hold fodder for horses.

A second well existed under the single storey front shop which it is understood was filled in after the sale of the property in the late 1970`s.

From 1923 onwards H A Hann used half of the shop area for a tinsmith`s shop. On market days farmers would buy his own produced milk buckets, chicken troughs etc.

The chimney in the dining room was of circular construction and the foundations consisted of gravel compacted. The structure of the building was half timbered with thin bricks of about one and a half inches thick. Some lower walls were constructed of three thicknesses of brick and two tiles on edge resulting in a solid wall of about eighteen inches depth. The timbers were of old oak, said to be old ship timbers.

The first extension to the building was carried out in 1936 and a further extension to the rear constructed in about 1960. All of the new extensions together with one room width of the old building now comprises number 36A College Street".

After finally moving into No 36 Harry set about enlarging his business the details of which will follow in another chapter. After a time Florence and daughter May decided to make use of the single storey extension to the front of No 36 and opened a general store selling groceries etc. I can just remember the store being open into the early 1950`s and would love to play with the display packets of Lyons Tea if allowed into the shop.

One story from the very early days of my childhood concerns my cousin Raymond Fiander and myself. When my mother took me in an afternoon to see my grandparents Ray would often come in from No 36A to play. The dining room table was a very large oval piece of furniture to which could be added up to two additional sections if required. We would set up our camp under this table and from the shop obtain a bottle of fizzy drink each called Or-Lem together with a packet of Smiths crisps complete with their small packets of salt in blue paper. All would be well for the young campers until the enevitable happened; one of us would forget the table above us and stand crashing a head on the heavy woodwork. Tears would abound and that would be the end of the picnic. Even in our sixties Ray and I laugh at ourselves to this day.

No 36 College Street was a very desirable property with three bedrooms in its final form, a large bathroom, a front reception room, good sized kitchen and a very large main living room which could easily accommodate about twenty seated people if required. The focal point was the large fireplace which was at some time reduced in size to look more modern. A large window at one end looked out into the garden and another smaller window looked into Florence's shop. This window would once have looked out towards College Street across a front garden and to the well, before the shop was built. Adjacent to the window was the long sealed up remains of the half door where perhaps the home brewed beer would have been sold in previous years.

Much of one wall within the main room was taken up by the curve of the drying funnel. On the opposite side of the room the stairs to the first floor rose firstly within the room before passing through a draft excluding door to continue the rise to above. These stairs were to be the cause a serious accident for Harry (snr) in his later years.

The oval dining table took centre position in the room complete with four large William IV chairs which remain with me today. Finally as in all religious victorian principle houses of stature the harmonium organ stood proudly in the corner watched over by a portrait size picture of Harry's hero the Liberal Prime Minister William Ewart Gladstone. Sadly the harmonium was disposed of soon after Harry's death together with Gladstone.

One additional room was the pantry / larder which was situated off the main room at the back of the house. This room was large enough to be made into another kitchen in twenty first century dimensions, but with a terra cotta tiled floor it was very cold in winter and remained cool throughout the summer. Good for milk, vegetables etc.

Until my parents took over the house there was no heating other than the warmth generated from the main room fireplace. Hot water to the hot water tank in the bathroom came from a small boiler in the workshop area.

The house was said to have been five hundred years or more old when purchased by Harry. It is very much of traditional oak beam structure and would have been half timbered on the College Street facarde. Hanging tiles now cover the first floor wall area with brick and some stucco at the lower level. From the noise of traffic at the front the rear garden presents tranquility with the large lawn near to the house where croquet was played in the nineteen twenties up to the nineteen fifties. At the further end of the lawn from the house fruit trees were in the lawn with early crop, Bramley and Blenheim Orange trees. In other areas there were pear and plum trees although by the nineteen fifties these were removed because of disease or produced inedible fruit.

A raised lawn above the rockery marked the start of the large vegetable growing area. This area would have been about the size of two allotment areas today and would have paid a vital roll in the production of food for the family. To complete the food growing area a large chicken run was established which during the second world war at least saw the addition of two geese.

To the side of the garden was a large greenhouse and some small building which could well have been part of the old bake house remaining after its demolition.

When No 36A was developed from No 36 a line from front to back of the garden passed to the new house. A privet hedge divided the properties from the house line to the top lawn which remained open to each house. Beyond this the two vegetable gardens were divided by a grass path always known rather obviously as the "middle path". A single width vehicle access was provided through the land of No 36A to No 36 arriving onto the lawn, but this was resited to cross into No 36 running parallel to the top lawn.

Florence and Harry enjoyed their home at College Street, but certainly did not have an easy time bringing up a family of five. Harry worked hard to make his money and Florence was diligent in seeing that every penny earnt was well spent on the essentials of life. To sew up every hole or tear in a garment was essential. New clothes were not cheap and started as Sunday clothes before demotion. There were days when it was not known where the next weeks food would come from.

Doris was the first to be married in 1926. She had taken a position as a milliner for a shop in the High Street in Gillingham, Dorset and had met her future husband Jack Ozzard at the Baptist Church. Jack would probably have called himself a plumber by trade, but he was much more than that. Working with his father much of Jack`s work was in Gillingham and the surrounding villages all within the farming area of North Dorset. The requirements of the people in Dorset would have been very similar to the requirements of people in Hampshire which meant that both Harry and Jack would often be called upon to go beyond basic plumbing producing sheet metal items, agricultural specialities etc. as required by the customer. Problem solving became a greater part of both of their working lives.

In another era Jack would have excelled in more complex and perhaps electronic fields as he could make "something from nothing". I was always in awe of him. He built his own lathe, constructed a utility type estate body for an Austin 7 car which lasted for many years, built a bungalow for his family in Gillingham which still exists, made up a camera from parts found at the local environmental dump to name but a few items.

After their marriage Doris and Jack lived in Gillingham for the rest of their lives having two children Roy, born in 1928 and Audrey born in 1934. Sadly Audrey died in May 2010, but Roy, now in his eighties, lives in nearby Shaftesbury where Audrey and her husband Alan Appleby also lived. Roy`s wife, Cynthia, sadly died in the 1986. Each have children and grandchildren many of whom live in the Shaftesbury area.

Evelyn was the second to be married to a local Petersfield man Herbert (Bert) Fiander. Bert was a very popular man born in Petersfield and worked most of his life for the Portsea Island Mutual Co-operative Society. He was a friend of the family before he married Evelyn having been a baker's roundsman after leaving school. Over the years he advanced within PIMCO to finally being the Petersfield representative selling the co-operative vouchers to local people. These could be later converted to a dividend payment for puchasing in Co-operative shops. By carrying out this work for many years he was well known in the town and had a considerable knowledge of the area and its people. Always happy his friendliness was infectious to all who knew him.

During the second world war Bert became a policeman in Petersfield. It would be fair to think of him as being similar to the 1950's BBC television series policeman, Dixon of Dock Green with Jack Warner. One of the "Old School". A job to do and a job to do properly without distraction. An ejected bomb from an enemy plane caused him considerable deafness from this time although it took many years of hinting from family before he succummed to wearing a hearing aid.

In 1936 the layout of 36 College Street was altered and extended to construct No 36A becoming Evelyn and Bert's home for many years. Only in their last years did they move from College Street to Gloucester Close in Petersfield.

Evelyn and Bert had three children, Robert (Bob), Barbara and Raymond. Bob lives with his wife Ruth at Parkstone, Poole in Dorset, Barbara lives with her husband David Hutchings at Kingston-upon Thames and Raymond lives with his wife Hilary in Echenevex, France. Each have children living in England and in France and Switzerland.

As in all families in Britain the coming of World War Two had a dramatic effect on the family. Although Harry snr. Jack and Bert were over the age of conscription all took up additional duties in the war effort. Harry snr. gave time and the experience learnt from his father to carry out the duties of undertaker in Petersfield and Bert became a policeman. Most of Harry's work involved the internment of townspeople who had died naturally, but an unforgetable time when he came very near to the horrors of war was when he carried out the final duties for some of those killed when a Nazi bomb hit the luckily empty air raid shelter and nearby buildings in Love Lane, Petersfield. He once told me that he had to prepare people for burial, but the details were something which remained personal to him for the remainder of his days.

All through the war Harry maintained his business of plumber and tinsmith as well as his undertaking duties. This eventually had an effect on his health such that the last years of the war were very hard indeed.

Reality came to the family when just before the outbreak of war Harry jnr. joined the local Territorial Army. On 3rd September 1939 Florence and Harry's son became a full time soldier with so many other men and women. Not until 1945 did my grandparents have their family safely at home again.

Gwen joined the Land Army and gave her time to producing the much needed foodstuffs for the country. During the early part of the war a young surveyor came to Petersfield to work for the local Urban District Council at the Town Hall. His name was Wilfred George from Bude in Cornwall. He stole the heart of Gwen and they married in 1941. After the war their homes were made in several parts of Somerset and Wiltshire and their final years were in Yeovil where my great grandfather had lived many years before. Wilf had worked for some time after the war with the Taunton building company Woolaways Construction and had become very much involved with the building of concrete sectional houses that were installed all over the country during the 1940s / 1950s. His calling however was to the church and during the 1950s he became a minister in the Congregational Church passing into the United Reform Church on the amalgamation of the Congregational and Presbyterian Churches. Canninngton, Bradford-upon-Avon, Stoke-sub-Hamden and finally Yeovil were his churches in his keeping.

Gwen and Wilf adopted a son Bryan around 1959 who still lives in Yeovil. A person with an adhesive character who loves his life and is an enjoyment to be with. Very much loved by all his cousins he is the youngest member of the Hann family cousins. Bryan is just Bryan.

Gwen passed away in 2001 and Wilf died in 2008 having passed the 90 age.

May had never married and had spent her life helping Florence in the shop and had taken her place as a lay preacher and a stalwart in the Methodist Church. She had many friends in the town, even now I have in my possession post cards from the 1930`s and 1940`s from her many friends on their travels. Sadly she did not find the romance that her sisters and brother found.

She suffered from Diabetis in a time when medical knowledge was not available as it is today. Subsequently it was necessary to have two of her toes removed. I can just remember her showing me the new spaces on her foot after the operation when I was a very small boy.

May died in 1950 from the complications of her illness.

My grandparents and the family were regular churchgoers and as there was no Baptist Church in Petersfield they initially attended the Congregational Church in College Street. At some time a difference of opinion caused them to transfer to the Primitive Methodist Church in Windsor Road. Here they became very much part of the community enjoying the church and its teaching. Over a period of time Harry snr., Harry jnr., May and brothers-in-law Bert and Jack became lay preachers followed in later years of course by Wilf and cousins Audrey and Roy. This must have been something of a record for the family.

Harry snr`s. preaching was very much of the victorian evangelical style. With very few notes his prayers were not short and were very much personal to those around him. His sermons were also from few notes and were very well received (and understood) by the small town and village people that he was speaking to. Common sense talking to ordinary people made him very popular, but a cushion between you and the hard chapel seat was a neccessity.

The amalgamation of the Methodist Churches in 1932 (Primitive, Wesleyan and United) saw the enforced closure of the smaller Windsor Road Chapel and the move to Station Road Chapel in 1941. This was not liked by many people and more than one generation passed before the "wounds" were healed. Even as a small boy I remember comments such as "it`s not like the Prim days" being uttered by discontented worshippers. Some people could not accept the amalgamation and left Methodism for other churches or gave up regular churchgoing altogether. A sad period for the church.

For the family the new church was a new challenge. They all became part of the united church undertaking a number of positions lay preaching or as part of the administration of the community. In many cases this continued with their children in future years.

The United Petersfield and Haslemere Circuit consisted of churches in Petersfield, Haslemere, Midhurst, Grayshott, Liss, Bowyers. Walderton, East Meon, Stroud, Stedham, Charlewood, South Harting and Buriton. With the exception of the main churches in Petersfield and Haslemere the country churches relied very much on the services conducted by lay preachers and in this area the family were very much commited to their church.

My grandmother, Florence or Nanny as I called her passed away in 1957 at the age of seventy seven after some years of failing health. As I was only twelve at the time some memories are a little clouded. I can remember her as a very quietly spoken lady who on more than one occasion would have cause to tell me off for being a somewhat noisey youngster. She was, I must admit, very right to do so.

Following a beach accident when she was young her left leg would not bend at the knee thereby giving her a "stiff leg". This meant that she could not walk around as others and usually had to be taken everywhere by car. On resting she would always rest her leg on a hassock or the former milking stool which had been adapted with a circular hassock type cushion on the top. The stool now devoid of the hassock top which was passed keeping remains in my house today in its first state as a miking stool.

Florence was able to visit Doris and Gwen and would visit family members and friends locally in Petersfield.

My memories of my grandfather Harry known to me as "Pop" were more vivid as after my grandmother`s death my parents, Jeff and I moved from Station Road to the house at 36 College Street. My grandfather had fallen down the stairs just before Florence had died and had crushed the Vertebrae in his back. This gave him much pain in his later life and restricted his movement considerably. The caring that he would need was in the majority provided by my mother and father with assistance from my aunt Evelyn at times. Despite the accident Harry was approaching eighty and needed general help in the large house. Also the business had grown and daytime answering of the telephone and callers queries became the duty of my mother.

During the six years living in the same house I got to know my grandfather very well. Perhaps we understood each others sense of mischief for one reason. Not only was he my grandfather he became a friend and mentor. When my father became authoritarian towards me he would mediate and peace would be restored. When my brother and I fought as brothers do he would mediate and when I brought my girlfriends home he would love to talk with them even though I wanted to take them out. There was nothing more infuriating than having to wait for a girlfriend who was chatting with your grandfather. "She`s going out with me, not you".

He told me much about his childhood and young life in Bournemouth and showed me how to make things in the workshop.

I remember one Saturday when he was confined to his bed with severe pain from his fall we just chatted about his life, his beloved Florence, his religious beliefs and much more. The details I cannot remember, but the day I remember well. So personal between grandfather and grandson.

My father together with the rest of the family had impressed on Harry that he should not drive his car again—the Ford Anglia, black of course, registration number LHO 445—as the roads were becoming busier and more dangerous. A nodding acceptance was all that we would ever get. One afternoon while everyone was out he got into his car and drove up over Stoner Hill to Hedge Corner, along the A32 to West Meon Hut and back along the A272 into Petersfield. Parking the car he made sure that he was back in his chair by the time everyone came home. At teatime he calmly layed his driving licence on the table and said to my father, "send this back to Winchester" (surrender this to the Hampshire licencing office at Winchester).

From the first trip in Bournemouth in the Peerless, around the south, east and west of England the driving days of this first generation driver were at an end.

Harry loved sport and in particular football. For many years he was president of the Petersfield United Football Supporters Club and annually presented the Hanna Cup to the winners of the Petersfield—v—Liss cup tie. He also supported Portsmouth and went to Fratton Park regularly by charabanc and by tram (Horndean and Portsmouth Light Railway) before the second world war. In later years the television provided his sport entertainment including boxing, horseracing, cricket and his beloved football.

Harry had always voted Liberal from days well before the second world war. Much to my mother's annoyance a portrait size picture of William Gladstone hung over Harry's favoured harmonium in the main room at College Street. Never would he allow the picture of his hero to be removed. but needless to say one day soon after his death the picture disappeared from its home never to be seen again. I think my mother may have known something about that !

Harry snr. slowly came to the end of his life and died on January 2nd 1964 at the age of eighty five, the same age as his father. Well known in Petersfield his funeral service was held in the Methodist Church attended by many friends and relatives. Finally he was laid to rest in the town cemetery alongside his beloved Florence and daughter May. The long journey had reached its end !

I was closer to grandfather Harry than to any other grandparent primarily because we had lived in the same house for several years. Even today I feel that his presence and his example has had a major influence on my life.

By the location address of the photographer and the age of the lady I can only
assume that this is a photograph of my grandmother Florence aged
about twenty two.

Harry snr engagement letter when he left Victoria Engineering at Sudbury, Suffolk and went to G J Hawkes at Hungerford in August 1904

G. J. Hawkes,
Ironmonger

Hungerford,
11th June 1909.

This is to certify that. H'y. Hann
has been in my employ
for. 5. years, during which
time I found him perfectly
honest, sober, + a good
workman, + always tried to
do his best for me. He has a
good all round knowledge of the
trade. His reason for leaving
me is, that this town does not
suit his wife's health.
I wish him every success.

Geo. J. Hawkes

A letter of recommendation from George Hawkes of Hungerford dated 16th
May 1909 when Harry left his employ to move to Cobham,
Surrey to work for Mr Allsworth.

A very early Hann family photograph in the garden of 36 College Street, Petersfield. Possibly taken around 1923 / 1925 with Harry snr. and Evelyn standing and May, Florence and Doris seated with Gwen and Harry jnr. standing.

The two Harrys` father and son photographed around 1925.

The family photograph at Florence and Harry`s fiftieth wedding celebrations at College Street. Standing from the left are Evelyn, May and Gwen whilst seated L-R are Harry jnr., Harry snr., Florence and Doris.

Many photographs of members of the family were taken in the garden of 36 College Street over the years and this one I feel is the most significant with regard to the family hence I have not tried to digitally repair the image.

Also at the fiftieth wedding anniversary celebrations were the grandchildren of the time posing here with their much loved grandparents.

From the left. Roy and Audrey Ozzard from Gillingham, Dorset, myself being held firmly by Harry snr., Raymond Fiander in front of Florence with Barbara and Bob Fiander to the right. This photograph has always been a favourite in the family and adorned the wall of most of the family houses for many years.

Of the group of grandchildren, Audrey passed away in 2010, but at the time of publishing the remainder are intact.

In later years the cousins became eight with the addition of my brother Jeffrey and Bryan George from Yeovil. Memories of our family childhood are talked about to this day.

A photograph of all the ladies of the Hann family taken at Florence and
Harry's fiftieth wedding celebrations.

From the left. Evelyn, May, Florence, Doris, Gwen and Ena.

The dresses would have been deemed upto date in the 1950's. To compare
with 2011 Evelyn would have been in her early fourties, May in her fifties,
Florence had passed her seventieth birthday, Doris was in her fifties, Gwen was
approaching her fourties and Ena in her early thirties. How times have changed!

A view of the garden at 36 College Street from my bedroom window looking
west towards King George Avenue. Apple trees are central with the gap
in the hedge still visible before construction of the new driveway and
garages at the end of the garden.

The churn tinning shed is visible to the right.

From just before the line of the first trees the whole area to the top of the
garden is now built upon.

A view from the top of the garden at 36 College Street looking towards the house. The gable end of the rear of 36A College Street is seen to the right.

This photograph was taken by me soon after the new driveway was constructed passing beyond the first two trees and then running off view to the left to the garage block.

The vegetable garden has been cleared and the new greenhouse would soon be constructed where the rubbish is piled.

The neighbouring corn stores to the left was demolished in later years. Note the stacks of milk churns ready for re-tinning or for eventual scrapping.

The whole of the garden to within about two metres of the house has now disappeared beneath a development of flats and apartments being sold by the family by the mid 1970's. Lost and gone forever.

Three sons-in-law of Florence and Harry snr.

From the left, Jack Ozzard married Doris, Bert Fiander married Evelyn and
Wilf George married Gwen. All pictured in the garden at
36 College Street, Petersfield

The three surviving Hann girls pictured at Gillingham, Dorset during the 1950`s / 1960`s with Doris on the left, Evelyn centre and Gwen on the right.

The bungalow behind was built by Doris`s husband Jack Ozzard with some help from his son Roy and still stands today. With no prior building knowledge Jack relied on a builder friend to keep an eye on his work as it progressed. Located on the road into Gillingham from Shaftesbury and adjacent to the railway line it was in a particularly good place for those interested in trains.

MY FATHER HARRY HANN JNR

After four girls both Florence and Harry had almost given up having a son, then on 10th March 1919 their prayers were answered and their son was born. Florence would have accepted the birth of her son in her normal quiet, loving way. For Harry all the normal father / son activities of the future would have been on his mind. From birth Harry jnr. was going to be spoilt somewhat by his parents and sisters something which would develop with a negative matter in future years.

Although Harry jnr was born at No 34 College Street the family moved into No 36 in 1923 so his main home was always considered as No 36. With a large garden and a rambling medieval house his early days were happy in such a large home. At a very early age he would love to go into his father's workshop to watch him and to play with all manner of tools. Undoubtedly Harry snr would show his son all kinds of jobs that he carried out secretly hoping that this would be the next owner of the business.

At five Harry started school at the Petersfield Junior School in St Peters Road meeting many new friends who would remain known to him for the remainder of his life. After all few people moved away from their home town in the 1920's unlike the later part of that century when to travel was an accepted and vital part of progression in life.

From the age of eleven Harry jnr. attended the Petersfield Senior School also in St Peters Road where he remained until he was fourteen. One of the teachers at this school was a very young Mrs Chapman who had the pleasure of teaching me when I attended the same school from 1957. Why did I have the feeling that at times she was looking at me and thinking "just like his father"?

On leaving school at the age of fourteen Harry jnr. headed in one direction, to work with his father. After all he would already have been halfway through his apprenticeship as Harry snr would have been guiding him for many years. The area of work would have been mainly in Petersfield with the occasional excursion to the outer villages of Buriton, Harting, Hill Brow, Rake, Steep Marsh, Steep and Stroud. With no car being owned all transport was by cycle carrying a boat shape canvas tool bag. Rain or shine this was the way to work in the 1930`s. The first motorised vehicle obtained was a Morris Cowley purchased for £17/10s (£17-50) sometime around 1937. Harry snr. did not have a driving licence and was not made to take a driving test, but Harry jnr. took his test at Winchester on July 3rd 1937 following a change in the law, his test would have been one of the earliest to take place in Hampshire.

Harry jnr. received a quite thorough teaching from his father not only in plumbing, but also sheetmetal work, leadwork and perhaps rather surprisingly in locksmithing. Many customers would come to the father and son as they knew that whatever they would overcome their problem in the fields practiced.

Harry jnr`s teenage years were typical of rural England in that time. With his family he became part of the Primitive Methodist Church in Windsor Road leading to the taking up of Lay Preaching towards the end of the 1930`s. He also learnt to play the violin and joined the PIMCO Band run through the Portsea Island Mutual Co-operative Society and on more than one occasion played at concerts in the old Corn Exchange in The Square, Petersfield. With Harry snr he became a supporter of Petersfield United Football Club and occasionally made the journey by charabanc and tram to Portsmouth to watch Pompey play.

Whilst at school Harry jnr had noticed a pretty dark haired girl from Weston called Ena Hiscock. One day whilst walking near the railway station in Petersfield he looked away from the direction that he was walking and promptly walked into Ena almost knocking her over. This was to be the start of a very long friendship and subsequent marriage although at the time Ena did wonder what sort of man this was having no regard for other people on the pavement. The date, November 27th 1937.

In the late 1930's Harry joined the local Territorial Army at the Drill Hall in Dragon Street, Petersfield little knowing of what was to happen over the next few years.

September 3rd 1939 was a day that would change the world not only for Harry jnr. and the family, but also for everyone else in Petersfield, England, Britain and the whole world. Never would life be the same again. On September 1st Harry jnr.was in uniform as 1455841 Bombardier Hann, 276 Battery 59th Anti Tank Regiment and "camping" at the Drill Hall in Dragon Street, Petersfield. In a few days he was sent to Burley in the New Forest before going to Torrington in North Devon. Whilst at Torrington and later in Bideford having a driving licence he was given a V8 engined American Buick car and told to take as many soldiers as could be carried and to teach them to drive. Many military personel at that time had not come from homes having a car so the duty given to Harry jnr. was vital to the war effort. In his own words Harry very much enjoyed exploring North Devon carrying out this chore, finding hitherto unknown places as Clovelly, Bude, Holesworthy, Barnstaple, Croyde and Ilfracombe. More like a holiday than fighting the war. Later on the army realised what was going on and exercised fuel restrictions on the project.

The time in North Devon played an important part in our family life as Bideford became an unofficial "second home" for us with many holidays being spent there in the 1950's and 1960's. Several friends were made particularly at the two Methodist Churches in the town. One lifelong friend was Henry Chubb who in 1946 became Mayor of Bideford. Each year we would visit Henry in his home. He had lost an arm in the First World War and had taken up local politics as a Labour Councillor. On the wall of his lounge was a picture of a Southern Railway West Country Class locomotive with many signatures at the bottom. Henry was Mayor when number 34019 "Bideford" was brought to the town for "christening" by him in his official capacity following which he was allowed to drive the engine (under control) within the railway goods yard. As a gift Henry was presented with a coffee table with the coat of arms of the Southern Railway on the top.

Henry had one daughter Rennie who married and had one daughter June. Hopefully those two items of railway history have been retained by the family. I can think of one person in Kent who would love to have that picture on the wall.

From North Devon Harry jnr. was moved to Lewes in Sussex where his group took over the old Navy Prison as a base. From here Harry`s duties were to support the defence guns at Newhaven and along the coast to Pevensey. For some time the grounds of Firle Place were also used as a camp. The Navy Prison in Lewes has long since been demolished, but during the early 1970`s I was involved with the construction of new ambulance and fire stations in the town and enquired from a local man as to where the prison had been. To my surprise and later to my father`s the ambulance station that I was helping to build was on that very site.

Campsell, Yorkshire and Kings Langley, Hertfordshire were further areas that Harry jnr. visited before being posted to Colchester in Essex.

Any leave would bring Harry jnr. back to Petersfield to see Ena and his family. Should Harry snr. be able to accumilate sufficient petrol ration tokens and be sure where Harry jnr. would be the family car would be loaded and visits made. Such were the travelling restrictions that the New Forest and Sussex were the main areas travelled to. Ena did however visit Kings Langley and Colchester by train.

The looming certainty that Harry jnr. would soon be going abroad hastened the wedding day for Harry jnr. and Ena and on 31st July 1941 they were married at the Primitive Methodist Church in Windsor Road, Petersfield. This was to be the last wedding ever to be held at the church, Brother-in-Law Wilfred George was best man and Barbara Fiander and Audrey Ozzard were bridesmaids. Harry was twenty one and Ena was twenty.

In the twenty first century weddings are still a big event, but unlike 1941 a great deal of money is usually spent by both families and the planning takes years not days as in Harry and Ena`s day. Many other couples wanted to marry before one or both were posted abroad and similar to this couple the reception was held in the family home with much of the cooking being the duty of the ladies of the family. Number 36 College Street was the ideal venue with its large garden. No time for an exotic honeymoon, it was back to barracks to carry on the job.

On 10th November 1941 Ena celebrated a quiet twenty first birthday. It was this day also the troopship Empress of Japan (later renamed Empress of Scotland) sailed down the River Mersey out of Liverpool heading for India. Harry jnr. was on board. Stops were made In Sierra Leone, West Africa and Durban, South Africa before arriving in Bombay (now Mumbai) and then to the initial base camp at Jhansi in Central India. The tour of duty took Harry to Dimapure, Shillong in Assam, Imphal and to Meiktila in Burma as part of the 14th Army, 17th Indian Division.

For Harry to see this new world of India, Burma and Assam made a deep impression on his life not only at this time, but for the remainder of his life. He saw povety that he could not have imagined in rural Hampshire. The family in Petersfield may have had to survive on the minimum of money, but these people survived daily on what food they could find from their own cultivation and the minimal money made from working for others who may have been wealthier than themselves. It came as no surprise therefore that the Indian continent peoples offered to work for the British Military even if that meant carrying out the meanest and lowest of duties. Cleaning and providing food and drink were two services carried out. Whatever the social feeling the support and hard graft of these peoples had a major effect on the success of the war.

The battle was made more difficult by the hilly terraine and jungle like plains. Furthermore when the monsoon season came everyone lived in mud and were soaking wet. Each hill had to be taken from the enemy and there seemed to be so many of those hills. As Transport Sergeant Harry`s duty was to provide the transport to and from the front. Hills, dales, rain, mud were not excuses, only challenges. Each fighting group did have one item of strength however in the form of a detachment of Ghurkas. These outstanding soldiers would often be told the objective and be left to their own means to rid the area of the enemy. From a very early age my brother and I were told about these soldiers and left in no doubt of their bravery. Our deep respect for them remains to this day without reserve.

On 28th March 1945 when the war in Europe was drawing to a close the fighting in Burma was still in a crucial stage. Harry was still at Meiktila at this time and very much fighting for survival. An exploding shell sent shrapnel in all directions. Harry was hit in the face below his left eye. Evacuated from the fighting Harry was taken to a hospital in Monywa where attempts were made to remove the metal, but without success. He was flown to Calcutta for more treatment, but for him the war was over and he would soon be returning to England. Secundrabad in South India was his last stopping place before setting sail for home through the Suez Canal and The Mediterranean arriving in England in June 1945.

Although not now being of grade one standard as a soldier he was still in the army and was based at Woolwich Baracks in South East London. Whilst Harry snr. tried to get his son demobbed due to his own failing health and the impact this was having on the family business the authorities were unmoved and Harry remained At Woolwich. With the end of the war in Europe many restrictions were lifted which meant that it was easier for Ena to visit Harry and the weekend leave was reality. For a time Ena lived with Harry in a room at 105 John Wilson Street, Woolwich at around February 1945.

On 9th March 1946 Harry was officially demobbed and placed on the reserve list. Ten days later disaster struck when his second (good) eye failed and he was admitted to the Cambridge Military Hospital in Aldershot with Cyclitis. The treatment was succesful in restoring his sight and he was discharged on 29th March although remained an outpatient until 11th May.

Although demobbed in March 1946 Harry remained on the reserve list from 18th June 1946 until 14th November 1953 when he was officially discharged. The Burma Star was included in his campaign medals.

Although married to Ena in 1941 only now would their life together begin with their first baby very near to making an arrival.

A much damaged school photograph with Harry jnr. in the front row, third
from left. The boy who is second from the left is George Rushmer who lived
in Petersfield all his life and whose son Gordon was in my class throughout
my schooldays. Gordon is an accomplished painter with water colours and (in
2011) was invited to show one of his paintings at a water colour exhibition
within the Tate Britain Gallery in London.

A wartime military photograph with Harry jnr. seated at the far left
on the front row.

Other Petersfield men in the photograph are Bob Williams, back row, sixth
from the left and "Tug" Wilson, front row, second from right.

One other person who remained a family friend for may years was "Curly" Cox,
front row, third from left who later married and moved to Exeter opening a
butchers shop in the city. If a family holiday took us to Exeter we would always
visit Curly and his wife Babs.

MY MOTHER, ENA

My mother's birth at ten past one on 10th November 1920 just thirty minutes after her sister Alma together were the first born of Thirza and Charlie joining Horace from Thirza's first marriage. The arrival three years later of Cecil made the family complete.

Life within the family in rural Hampshire at that time has already been recorded, but Ena was quite an independant person of quiet disposition not having the "love life" character of her sister and younger brother. This would bring some friction at times between them and it could have been said that Ena was "a bit of a loner".

Loyal to her family she would often visit her grandparents, aunts and uncles in the area as well as to her not so close relatives Sid and Nell Chitty and their children Margo and Jean at the limeworks cottages on Butser Hill. The daily walk to school initially in Buriton and in later years in Petersfield with brothers and sister and walks up onto Butser, Wardown and Haydown above Buriton was something she would relate to me as a child many times.

Leaving school at the age of fourteen she became employed in domestic service at Wardown House near Buriton Cross Roads together with Alma for Paymaster Rear Admiral Herbert Gyles. Ena's medical card dated 1937 confirms that Wardown was her home address, but the Admiral died on October 4th 1937 leaving a widow and a daughter so it is most likely that the employment would have ceased soon after.

Within some of her effects remaining with me after she died was a small photograph album from that time which had belonged to the Gyles family. It contained many photographs from 1936 of the house and views towards the Downs. Much of the content of this album has been scanned and is in the possession of The Buriton Heritage. On the day the scanning was carried out I was introduced the the owners of the house at that time who presented me with a copy of the sales literature for the property when they purchased. In return I asked that the Heritage present them with a set of the pictures scanned from the album.

About 1938 Ena went to work for the general provison shop of Fullers at the junction of Chapel Street and Lavant Street in Petersfield as a shop assistant. In 1939 Ena was lucky to be able to obtain employment with F W Woolworths at their modern store in the High Street in Petersfield. New to the small towns Woolworths sold almost everything anyone would require for household use and to be accepted to work there was "good for the cv". As Ena had met Harry in 1937 there was obviously more than one reason for wanting to work in Petersfield.

Ena and Harry`s friendship grew and Ena became very much involved in the Hann family life and with the Methodist Church in Petersfield. The family move to 25 Tilmore Road and this saved Harry the walk or cycle ride to Weston. But war clouds were looming and Harry`s duty to the Territorial Army meant that their free time together was limited. It was in Woolworths one day in 1939 that Harry had to tell Ena that he had been called up into the full time army.

With Harry away in the army Ena`s life centred around her work, her own family, Harry`s family and the Methodist Church. If there was ever a chance to meet up with Harry she would travel as she could to see him within the ever tightening wartime restrictions. The call to carry out different jobs for the war effort saw Ena leave Woolworths and take factory work with Talbot Ponsonby Engineering at Langrish a few miles west of Petersfield. Shift work was demanded which meant that sometimes she would take the three mile ride to Langrish on a Hants & Dorset bus or if there was no service it meant that she would cycle the distance. Her fear was not the length or terrain of the journey as in normal conditions the roads were fairly quiet, but with the demands of war the proximity of the two major ports of Southampton and Portsmouth, the major army camps at Bordon and Longmoor meant that the road became a busy route with lorries and tanks with very new drivers who could only just master the controls to start and stop let alone to make allowances for girls on bicycles. I asked my mother once if she had any idea of what she made at

Langrish to which her answer was "lots of small things for aeroplanes". It was wartime so that was all she needed to know.

Working at Talbot Ponsonby`s gave the chance for Ena to make new friends. Some of those were men and women who had been working at the factory before the war started, others were "conscripts" like herself. It was essential to have time to laugh in such a time and practical jokes were commonplace. One story concerned an unnamed man who would leave his bicycle beside the emergency water tank situated in the grounds of The Railway Hotel in Petersfield whilst taking the bus to Langrish. His conduct towards his workmates left something to be desired so an unknown person not working one day ensured that the bicycle was well and truly washed by dropping it into the tank. On the return of the owner the bicycle was still swimming and remained that way for some time.

When it became known that Harry would be going abroad to fight wedding plans were made and Harry did his duty by asking Ena`s father for her hand in marriage. Initially my grandfather refused saying that he would not allow Ena to marry until she was twenty one. Sadness and disbelief at this decision they appealed to him to reconsider, but without success. Even Harry snr. went to Charlie and pleaded with him to think again about the situation that Harry jnr was going away to fight and may never return and his daughter only wanted to marry some four months before the age of twenty one. Eventually Charlie changed his mind and gave his blessing on the couple. The marriage was arranged for July 31st 1941.

One other factor which may well have changed Charlie`s mind was the same situation being presented by twin sister Alma and Wally Lamport who also was about to go abroad. Their response seemed more positive and they were married at St Peters Church, Petersfield on July 19th 1941.

After Ena and Harry`s wedding it was back to work, Harry to his army service and Ena to Talbot Ponsonby`s. A wedding present from her workmates at Langrish broke the law as far as the use of metals during that time. No questions asked the happy couple received six brass egg cups all chrome plated. These are extremely heavy for the job that they were made for and although they easily tarnish: they remain in my ownership to this day. Whereas the modern egg cup is light and often made in plastic these would inflict some damage if they were dropped onto ones toe.

On Ena`s twenty first birthday Harry was sailing down the River Mersey to India. Their married life together would not be a reality until 1946. Her home changed to 36 College Street with Florence, May and Harry snr. who gave great, but often silent strength to Ena over the next few years. In addition the presence of Evelyn and Gwen nearby helped during the bad times ahead.

Ena and Harry during the 1940's. Sgt. Harry in army uniform, a posed photograph of Ena and their wedding photograph of 1941.

MY PARENTS, ENA AND HARRY

To at last be able to return to Petersfield together in 1946 was a time of unimaginable happiness for Ena and Harry and for both families. For five years since their marriage they could not be together for any length of time, now they could at last build their home together and await the arrival of their first child namely myself. This came about on 17th June 1946 at Langtons House in Alresford. They had lived briefly at 12 North Road in Petersfield, but it is most likely that by the time of my birth the new family home had become a flat at "Esmonde", Ramshill, Petersfield. No longer standing, the large house became flats and later a small girls school before being demolished for the redevelopment of the first part of Madeline Road. In July 1948 this flat is recorded as being the residence of Ena and Harry.

Harry jnr. resumed working with his father and renewed friendships within the area. Ena became a full time "mum", but occasionally helped at 36 Collge Street as well as visiting her family home at Tilmore. The Methodist Church connection remained as strong as ever.

By April 1950 Ena and Harry had purchased numbers 28 and 30 Rushes Road and moved into number 30 whilst letting No 28 initially to Albert Andrews and family and later to Bob Whitewood and family. The house was a substantial edwardian three bedroom, two reception house with a traditional good size garden at the rear. Over the next few years they modernised the house within the constraint of post war austerity and grew vegetables in the garden. The addition of a greenhouse and a large cold frame provided tomatoes and salads for the summer period. As with the majority of urban gardens a few chicken were kept at the bottom of the garden for eggs and to sacrifice one chicken for the Christmas dinner. These were the days before frozen food was available for domestic consumption.

Wartime austerity had meant that if you wanted more than your ration of eggs you kept your own chicken and if you wanted fresh food you grew it. Likewise if you wanted to eat chicken you could buy with restrictions or you kept your own with a friendly cockerel to fertilise the eggs so enabling you to breed new chicks and keep the process running. The austerity covered not only foods, but also clothes so "mend and make do" was the order of the day. Austerity measures remained for some items until 1954 with the family Ration Book being the most treasured possession.

Few cars were parked in Rushes Road in the 1940`s and 1950`s so when old enough I could play with my friends in the street. Both bread and milk were delivered to the door and the familiar red Co-op van with Mr Lander at the wheel was eagerly awaited on delivery days. As I became older I was allowed to cross the A272 at the bottom of the road to gain access to the recreation ground with its swings, slide and roundabout. Although life at this time was quite hard in another way it was happy and carefree with children being able to play freely without problem.

Early in 1951 my mother told me the big secret that I would soon have a baby brother or sister and that it would arrive just about the same time as my fifth birthday. True to the story on June 23rd 1951 mother gave birth to my brother Jeffrey. According to my father, as I had been very good around the time of Jeff's birth I was to be taken on the train to London to see the Festival of Britain exhibition on the South Bank as a reward. My! this was to be the first of many many train journeys to London in my life. Of the day I can remember the general layout of the exhibition, the Skylon, an electric locomotive, the Festival Hall and the old Shot Tower. Looking across the Thames my father pointed out a London Transport Tram on the Embankment. Little did I realise that I would never see one again as this was to be the last year for trams in London.

Perhaps it was a reward or perhaps it was a form of bribery making that first trip to London as it was soon made fully aware to me that in September I was going to have to start school for the first time AND I would have to go there all day on Mondays through to Fridays. Not so good when you have spent the last five years at home playing all day with everything being done for you by mum and dad. This was no way to treat me surely? Alas, I was soon to be corrected and my time of education commenced at

Petersfield Junior School in Hylton Road where I was delivered daily and collected by my mother with occasional duties being carried out by my father. One respite was that I did not have to stay at school for dinners and usually went home to Rushes Road for my lunch although all journeys seemed a very long walk. Being five years old I was man enough for the treck whilst my little brother rode in his carriage (pram) beside. His day would come.

The Coronation of Queen Elizabeth II in June 1953 was a time for celebration everywhere. At number 30 Ena and Harry took the decision to invest in "one of those new televisions" so that we could watch the Coronation at home. Apart from a brief view of a small television as a very young boy at a house in Hampton Court, Surrey this was to be our first experience of something which would effect everyone's lives. As my grandmother had been born in Southend-on sea it was decreed that we should have a television made by E K Cole of the same town with the trade name "Ekco" and the Petersfield branch of Currys was selected to supply the machine with help for the aerial erection coming from the Southampton company, Belchers.

The main event day came and whereas early television broadcasts only took place from around 1930 until 2230 each day this important celebration was almost an all day event. Being all live there had to be a break during the day for staff to rest not least the commentator Richard Dimbleby who seems even now to have described every happening in detail for the whole day. Number 30 Rushes Road had a stream of callers that day all wanting to see the event.

Life seemed to be quite mundain for the next few years, school, school holidays, sunday school, visits to both my grandparents. Holidays initially were incorporated as visits to relatives the first for me being to Southend-on-sea, but South Yorkshire and Taunton also were seen. Around 1950 we borrowed the family Ford 8 and ventured to Westward Ho! in North Devon for the first of many holidays at Braddicks Caravan Site. Starting at 0830, dinner en route at Gillingham or Taunton arriving at Bideford by 1700 for a Hockings ice cream is imprinted in the minds of Jeff and myself. Every year there were visits to Clovelly, Ilfracombe, Croyde and Barnstaple as well as duty calls on at least three of my father's old 1939 friends, Henry Chubb, Reeny Chubb and Leonard Cock. So repetitive and yet we all looked forward to and enjoyed the holidays immensely.

As Jeff aged he was taught all the tricks and bad habits that had been learnt by his elder brother some of which backfired on me in later years. He will still give a very one sided version of the time that he walked on my father's treasured cold frame and found out that the glass would not take his weight. As the glass broke he fell through. I came to the rescue and pulled him clear. Unfortunately the top rear of his leg came in contact with a jagged edge of glass tearing a hole through the skin. Much blood and tears from Jeff as mum and dad came to find out what all the noise was about. Jeff went to hospital and I got a smack for not looking after him properly and for actually rescuing him. In todays light I should obviously have carried out a Risk Assessment before carrying out the rescue procedure, but to hell with that, he was my brother and he needed help!

In 1953 / 1954 a bungalow, "Rotherley", at number 2 Station Road became vacant. Mum had always loved the building from the outside and it was decided that the family would move there. Duly purchased by my father we all said goodbye to 30 Rushes Road little realising that many years later Jeff and his wife Lyn would purchase the property again as a family home.

The bungalow was truly a very nice property situated on the corner of Station Road and Oaklands Road. Set in its own grounds it was possible to walk all round the building or in the case of Jeff and myself to cycle all around. With two bedrooms, a lounge and a kitchen / diner it was of a good size for the four of us. Dad later built a brick garage and cultivated the very large garden. The rear garden had a number of apple trees, but in the front garden was a very large beech tree. First myself then Jeff conquered the towering timbers and not just once did it become a refuge for me after I had annoyed my father. Sadly both bungalow and tree no longer exist, but in the few short years that we lived there it was truly a home.

My interest in transport continued to be fuelled at Rotherley with a bus stop out side the gate for both Aldershot & District and Hants & Dorset incoming buses, the railway station just along Station Road and a continual procession of trucks and coaches from the Winchester and Alton directions adding to transport leaving the town. Could it ever get better?

In 1957 my grandmother Hann died leaving my grandfather alone in 36 College Street. Whether it had been decided in earlier years or whether it was decided just after Florence's death, we were to leave Station Road and move to College Street. My mother found it very hard to accept this. The bungalow was very much a home to her whereas 36 College Street was a large rambling tudor house with many corners and crevices. Walls were not straight or level and the whole place creaked as you walked through.

The move to College Street meant that Jeff and I became part of the H A Hann & Son structure. There was no part of the day that we could not see or hear something in the workshop or have contact with the employees. There was little escape as both Jeff and I were seen as "fair game" for practical jokes by them and who could have blamed them. The bosses two little angels asked for all they got from Charlie, Haden, Les and co.

During the remaining six years of my grandfather Harry's years we all lived very closely and sometimes this could inevitably lead to friction. My mother always remained rather bitter at having to leave Rotherley and this spun off into the daily round. Jeff at six sometimes found it rather hard to understand the peculiarities of the elderly and poor old dad was in the middle and so often the mediator. On the other hand I always got on very well with my grandfather and enjoyed just chatting to him as I have described earlier. The majority of meals were taken together which meant that my parents often had little time for themselves. Most summers Harry snr. would go to either Doris and Jack at Gillingham, Dorset or to Gwen and Wilf at Cannington in Somerset for a week's holiday and on some days an invite for him to eat at Evelyn and Bert's next door would allow a little freedom for us all. In his last few months my grandfather became increasingly bedridden, but always enjoyed visitors whether family or friends.

My father was a person that you would like or dislike. He would be seen as many as a very friendly and helpful person and by others as a rather rude, short tempered and unhelpful man with an air of high self importance. I could never say that I enjoyed a satisfying time with him, but in fairness we did have some good times together in later years. He could make, not enemies, but "non friends" quicker than he could make friends having been in his presence on a number of occasions when this took place. Very embarrassing and I could never understand why he had to upset people who only wanted to help him.

The lawn at 36 College Street was large enough to play cricket in and sometimes Jeff, my cousin Raymond Fiander and myself would set the stumps for a game. On one occasion Jeff and myself were playing after tea on a summer's evening. I was batting and Jeff bowling and as can be imagined I was settled at the wicket with poor Jeff endlessly bowling the ideal batsman's ball. After some time my father decided that I should be removed and took over the bowling from Jeff. Very soon I was "out" and father took his place at the stumps awaiting my bowling. First class cricket was seen on the lawn that day as my first ball met the bat and was propelled at high speed through the dining room window shattering glass across the room. My mother luckily was not or could not watch and ended up with her hair full of glass splinters whereas my grandfather had escaped narrowly from the passing ball.

As the ball hit the glass both Jeff and I departed at high speed up into the garden knowing full well that one or both of us were about to be blamed for the happening. I think the story was that it was my bowling that had caused my father to break the window. However Jeff and I melted into the vegetable patch laughing uncontrollably until we found courage to return to the house to see the damage and receive the wrath of our father's temper. This illustrates the uncertainty of my father's moods and how our lives could instantly be changed from happiness to sadness.

My mothers character was quiet and somewhat reserved, but particularly in later life we all realised that the real Ena had never been allowed loose. She had a good sense of humour and enjoyed friendship. However she would neither "spare the rod" or be slow to vent her feelings if any of us caused her to. Always one of the "back room people" at church events nevertheless she gave so much to the Methodist Church. Many people had experienced her excellent cooking and had seen her skills in flower arranging, but often had not known who was responsible for the enjoyment. Her cooking skills were aided by the much loved Rayburn solid fuel cooker at Rushes Road and Station Road followed by the supreme Aga cooker at College Street and thereafter King Georges Avenue. Food types were traditional and well tested. My first taste of curry was after I had met my wife in 1965 as it just wasn`t eaten in our household.

Very much a person of habit Jeff and I always knew what she was doing or where she had gone on any particular day of the week. To disrupt this was a major incident and instant decisions to call in to see someone were few and far between. To visit someone who was sick or in need she would almost always plan and pre-arrange the visit beforehand.

After our move to College Street mum spent much of the time looking after the showroom and telephone answering save for Tuesday and Friday afternoons when she would go shopping in the town. Many years passed before my mother-in-law pursuaded her to go to the Thursday afternoon ladies meeting at the Methodist Church. This meant the closing of the showroom at this time and from then on her weekly outing to the Womens Guild was an enjoyment and perhaps some regret that she had not gone earlier.

During the late 1960`s the rambling house at College Street had become too big for just Ena and Harry to live in. The requirement for a large workshop and stores had decreased after the end of the milk churn repairs and the reduction in the number of people employed. Material suppliers who at one time would only deliver once or twice per week now offered a far better frequency. In addition the facilities provided locally by Gammon & Smith had been expanded considerably catching up with the larger merchants in the Hampshire / West Sussex area. More items became "off the shelf" at Petersfield than ever before and if they were not available in store they were obtained very quickly. The hunt was on for a smaller house with or without a workshop or at least where one could be erected on the property. Eventually a property at the corner of King Georges Avenue and Station Road was rented. Some work was carried out to upgrade the empty three bedroom detached house with a view to perhaps being able to purchase at a later date, however this never came about so after a few years a further move was made to 22 Barham Road which was a property within site of the rental house.

Smaller, but more functional for Ena and Harry the house benefitted from the new Petersfield car park being built as this allowed them to obtain rear access to the garden and to construct a garage. Suddenly the houses in Barham Road became desirable town houses. During the period at Barham Road retirment for Harry was determined as detailed elsewhere. Both Ena and Harry were slowing down considerably and their last move was to be again within view of the house being sold. The flats and maisonettes in Winton Road were built along the new access road to the car park and it was to number 10 Winton Road that Ena and Harry made their last move. By the time this took place Harry had retired fully, but not many years would remain for them to be together.

The Methodist Church remained very much in Ena and Harry's lives for the remainder of their lives. Harry was a lay preacher for fourty two years and a Trustee of the church for almost as many years. Few weekends passed with Harry not taking a service at one or other of the churches in the Circuit. As time went by my mother, Jeff and I became very well known in the churches visited with my father. My father's services were very much basic non-conformist speaking in a language which was understandable by all people.

One event that took place every year was the Good Friday service at Buriton Methodist Church. I am not sure of when or where it came about, but it may have been a Hann family organisation from well before the second world war. The service consisted mainly of a concert of church music including anthems and readings the choir being made up of family members as well as one or two close friends from Petersfield Methodist Church.

Harry also became involved in the Petersfield Chamber of Commerce and remained in the organisation for many years. The Annual Trades Exhibition in the Town Hall was supported by him not only within the organising commitee, but also in the prime period of H A Hann & Son a stand was taken to show the services of the company. The provision of Christmas Lighting in the Square also came into his involvement and I remember well the time when he produced largely single handed sufficient lanterns made out of galvanised steel to hang all round the Square from posts secured against the old cattle rails. Hand cutting the conical tops, bases with holes to accommodate the bulb and batten holder and four corner sections took a great deal of time as did the assembly and painting before they were ready for the town to see. The Window Display Competition and the Carnival were also part of his interests.

Holidays as already stated were initially mainly to the west country. Not only the much loved Westward Ho!, but Paignton and Looe were visited. The occasional change took us to Llandudno, Walton-On-Naze (Essex) and Yorkshire. After I had removed myself for separate holidays mum, dad and Jeff extended the distances to include Scotland. After Jeff's departure holidays by coach were taken, but just one continental holiday was to Holland and a visit to the bulbfields. Both Ena and Harry's love of their gardens and in particular flowers ensured that this one trip was very much enjoyed. West Country holidays were still taken, but less and less as they became older.

As all families grew both Jeff and I married and left home, myself in 1967 and Jeff in 1971. My wife is Suzan Hall Hadland who came from Hove. Of our children, James now lives in Hove with his partner Julie and Lee lives in Oporto, Portugal with her husband Paulo and their children Sofia and Miguel. Jeff's wife is Marilyn (Lyn) Newman from Liss and their children are Samantha, Emma, Louise and Jessica.

The family story is brought to an end at this point because the details of the present day members of the family are known to those living. It is for others to continue from here.

Harry's health was moderate in the last of his years between retiring at the age of seventy, but his last few days were short and he died in hospital at Portsmouth on 24th November 1994 at the age of seventy five.

Ena showed signs of dementia very soon after Harry's death. This became more accute and she spent the last two and a half years of her life in good care at Rotherbank Nursing Home, Liss Forest where she died on 27th July 2001.

A group photograph of Ena and Harry jnr. at their wedding reception on 31st July 1941 in the garden of 36 College Street.

From the left, Harry snr., Florence, Audrey, Harry jnr., Ena, Wilfred, Barbara, Gwen, Thirza and Charlie.

A photograph of me in my first mode of transport in the garden of Esmonde, Ramshill, Petersfield in about 1947.

Prams then as now must carry far more than just a child. There was even a secret compartment under my feet no doubt for carrying contraband, cash or jewellery.

A photograph on the left of three generations in the garden at 36 College Street, Harry snr., Harry jnr. and myself. The date of the sitting was about 1947.

My mother and father Ena and Harry jnr. at Cheddar Gorge a year or so later on one of the first of our many holidays in the west country.

A very young me in the garden at 36 College Street, Petersfield with my cousin
Raymond Fiander. This long area of grass always remained without boundaries
between 36 and 36A College Street and was sometimes used for tennis games
within the family.

Note the ever present milk churns in the background.

Two Christmas photographs of the main room at 36 College Street showing my parents Ena and Harry jnr. with my brother Jeff and grandfather Harry snr.

The large table and chairs owned by my grandparents had given way to my parents wartime austerity standard table with four chairs with the matching sideboard to the right of both views. The sideboard is still in my possession although much modified to suit our present home.

The curve of the drying funnel provides the wall to the right and the "cricket ball window" to the garden is at the left top. It is not difficult to see how the path of the ball could have caused serious harm to either my mother or my grandfather.

My father did not eat all of the turkey, but I would have had a good go at eating most if not all of mum's Christmas cake.

Photographed in North Devon on holiday in the 1950's Ena and
Harry jnr. relax in the area they loved so much.

A unique photograph taken in the Methodist Church, Station Road, Petersfield.

When the amplification system was being installed the wiring was carried from one side of the church to the other by laying it across the roof support beams. This meant that the electricians involved had to gain access to the area high above the congregation seating. As far as I know this is a one and only photograph of the altar taken from this high level which was given to my father. Now somewhat altered the centrepiece of the church was a place that many generations of the Hann family would know well.

H.A. HANN & SON

The start of H A Hann, Plumber and Tinsmith at 34 College Street, Petersfield in 1913 was to have a significant effect on the whole of the Hann family for three generations. The prime mode of transport, the bicycle, travelled locally to Buriton, Harting, Hill Brow, Rake, Steep Marsh, Steep and Stroud with extention over a period of time to include Milland, East Meon and Froxfield. Petersfield town also provided an ever growing number of customers. It was not until 1937 that the first car was purchased. The move to number 36 College Street in 1920 gave Harry snr. a substantial workshop ideal for the tinsmithing part of the operation.

Over the pre war years Harry snr. was able to secure a number of important customers in the area including Alan Lubbuck of Adhurst St Marys, Sheet, Col. Bonham Carter of Buriton Manor, Admiral Sir Stuart Bonham Carter at The Heath, Petersfield and Dr Pankridge also at The Heath, Petersfield. He was very aware however that the nucleus of his fast growing clientele were the people of the town and local villages who warmed to him and gave him their support.

Whilst Harry`s main trade was plumbing he was a very skilful man particularly with regard to metalwork. Lead, copper and sheet steel were his main lines of talent. Few if any people passing through Petersfield Square today would glance in detail at King Williams hands. No-one would now remember that in the 1930`s Harry made and installed a new lead finger for the King replacing one which had been broken off. I remember my father "pointing" out the new finger to me as a young boy.

Harry snr. was aware that he needed some "Bread and Butter" work and approached The South Eastern Farmers milk dairy with regard to milkchurn repairs. Their interest and acceptance started a business relationship which was to last for fifty years. Every week, sometimes twice a week a churn lorry would draw up outside the workshop with a variable number of churns. These would be stacked on the roadside (then pavement when the roadway was upgraded) ready for Harry or one of the family to take inside. Any repaired churns would be placed outside earlier in the day or taken direct from inside the workshop by the driver and mate.

The heavy galvanised steel ten gallon churns of the post war time were small against the seventeen gallon churns that Harry snr. started his repair work with in 1913. Both had separate handles, top and bottom rims which if damaged had to be resoldered together before re-use. Soldering in the twenty first century usually means a small electric hand held iron whereas the irons used by Harry and successors had large copper bits with iron framework and wooden handle. To hold one of these monsters horizontally in one hand for more than a few minutes was impossible. To heat these irons Harry constructed a coke burning stove which was placed on the workshop bench with a paving stone below to protect the wooden bench from catching fire. A steel flue pipe rose from the fire through the workshop above and the rooftiles to emit its sometimes quite black smoke into the sky above College Street. At the front of the fire was an opening of about 300mm wide by 50mm high through which the iron was placed directly into the centre of the burning coke.

The ideal fire was a redhot glow, but the iron could not be overheated otherwise the soldering operation would fail. Harry`s skill and the skills of others in later years at knowing just the right time to extract the soldering iron cannot be described and is certainly not in any instruction book. Old skills, old ways.

After heating the iron was dipped in spirit of salts before being taken to the churn and repairing the damage with the help of a clean surface with the spirit and a liberal amount of solder melted off a solder stick. If all went well the holes were sealed, handles re-attached and rims secured. If any part of the process failed you started again.

The basic churn repair started as a job for Harry snr., but everyone who worked for the company was trained in the art as part of their job. Only in the late 1950`s and 1960`s was someone employed solely to repair the churns and also to carry out the "re-tinning" of churns. This was an old school and life long friend of Harry jnr., Les Marsh.

Some time during the 1950's a suggestion was made by South Eastern Farmers that the re-tinning of milk churns could be assigned to H A Hann & Son and the two Harrys subsequently visited the large dairy at Sturminster Marshall in Dorset to inspect their plant and watch the process taking place. A decision was made to go ahead with the support of SEF and a special corrigated asbestos building was constructed next to the large greenhouse in the garden at 36 College Street. Twenty first century Health & Safety Laws would not have accepted the plant in any way as little or no regard for the dangers of working with molten tin, hydrochloric acid etc. were adhered to or indeed understood as to their long term damage to the human body. This coupled with the building construction would not exist today.

The process commenced the day prior to the actual re-tinning process when a maximum of eight churns (by now all of the ten gallon size) were immersed into a rubber lined tank filled with 50% strength hydrochloric acid. The churns remained in the tank overnight and when removed they would be washed in Bakers Fluid and await dipping. All rims, handles etc. would be removed for re-fitting later although by now most handles were part of the top rim and not singularly removeable.

The tin had been heated from about 0700 on the day of tinning in the gas fired vessel and the process for each churn was to dip and revolve to ensure that all surfaces were recoated in the new tin. Considering the preparation time the actual process took just a few minutes, then to cool. The replacement of rims would be carried out in the main workshop in the days following before the churns would be ready for return to the Station Road dairy.

The fumes given off by the process were so obnoxious that the second hand windows fitted to the plant were always open during tinning. Many a time the prime man involved in the process would escape into the garden coughing heavily where my mother would hastily provide him with a glass of water. The situation was not aided in any way by Les Marsh's heavy smoking habit. Body protection consisted of a rubber apron and heavy rubber gloves primarily to avoid burning by acid or by molten tin. On reflection the trades once carried out in this form and accepted as normal bring shudders to the present day thinking.

Repairs and the retinning of milk churns continued until 1963 when South Eastern Farmers decided to close the wholesale milk processing at Petersfield leaving only a bottling facility at Station Road. The converted wartime Bedford Q lorries together with the Dennis Max and Pax and later Bedfords became just a memory for Petersfield folk. Their orange / red colours adorned Charles Street whilst waiting a drop off place in the dairy. The grey Scammell Highwayman tankers of United Dairies travelling several times a day to London were also gone for ever.

Plumbing and later the central heating work had continued to develop before the Second World War. Both father and son very much enjoyed their work, but Harry snr. found the wartime period particularly tough with the extra workload and applied to the military for Harry jnr`s early demobilisation at the end of hostilities. The request fell on deaf ears and coupled with the after effects of Harry jnr`s injury matters took their own time. Even at the age of seventy Harry snr. was still working much of the day. The death of his beloved Florence in 1959 followed by a fall resulting in a serious back injury determined the end of Harry snr`s working life. Although he would try to sit in the workshop on an improvised chair to repair milkchurns the resulting pain was too much to bear.

Harry jnr gradually took full control and the 1950`s became a period of growth for the company. The introduction of Local Authority Improvement Grants enabled many households without a bathroom to apply for a 50% Grant towards the conversion and extension of outbuildings to provide a modern bathroom. In most cases the conversion of the existing coal store, household washing room with its integral copper bowl for heating with a solid fuel fire to provide hot water for the clothes or similar attached structure became the basis for conversion. A window was added, new floor, new roof and direct access to the house via the kitchen before walls were plastered and painted before the sanitary ware was installed. A relatively cheap way of providing up to date facilities. Harry jnr. quickly took up the gauntlet and made this type of work a major part of the companies source of income. He would sell it as a package from assisting in the application for the Grant, providing plans for the Local Authority`s approval and then project manage the whole installation carrying out as much of the site works as possible. Messrs Suthers the electricians and Harold Winscome the plasterer were often employed for the projects.

Another major development took place in the early 1960's when the company was awarded the contract for plumbing and heating maintenance work previously undertaken by the direct labour force of Petersfield Urban District Council. Being unable to sustain the work load the Council had decided to employ a local company to carry out all works under an agreed price system. As part of a general process of upgrading the properties H A Hann & Son would carry out required works and report back any matters which would result in sudden breakdowns or which required early attention before problems arose. Depending on the weekly work load from one to four operatives were required to maintain the contract with direct instructions being received from the Council's Surveyors Department.

This contract proved to be very profitable for the company with local work and little pre-purchasing required. Many of the Reema concrete houses had replacement fireplaces / water boilers installed over a period of several years. The installation which commenced as a two day operation was gradually streamlined to two houses in three days especially when Billy Kates and myself were the work force.

As part of the 1974 local authority alterations both Petersfield Urban and Rural District Councils ceased to exist as did the same Councils at Alton. All services were brought under the banner of East Hampshire District Council and although the combined offices were eventually to be in Petersfield building services requirements were to change. Gradually more work was undertaken in house and the lucrative contract came to an end.

Expansion had taken place in the private sector from the 1960's extending the customer area to Alresford, Medstead, Farnham, Midhurst and Portsmouth. My entry into the company came over the hard winter of 1962 / 1963 and my brother Jeff arrived in 1967. The small showroom was well used for off the street customers as well as regulars and included tiled fireplaces and a bathroom layout. My mother Ena attended to the day to day visitors, telephone, and deliveries as well as maintaining the large house for us all. Little advertising was necessary as the name of H A Hann & Son was well known in the area. The order book was so often full with several weeks waiting list. The purchase of two Ford Anglia vans in 1962 and 1963 provided mobile advertising and the hang on sign board gave notice of the company's presence.

From just before the second world war it was necessary to obtain short term help to complete work. Bert Fiander would sometimes assist the two Harry's when he was not at his work particularly during the war when Harry jnr.was away. A number of men from the area were employed for a period of time as follows:

John Lancaster, later to enter the Elim Church and become their most senior leader.

E Albuery
Harold Marsh
Haden Dodd, one of the longest serving plumbers working under both Harry's as his boss.
Charlie Kates, remained with the company for seventeen years before starting his own plumbing business.
Bill Kates, Charlie's son joined the company after leaving school and followed his father to their own business.
Les Marsh, at school with Harry jnr. and joined primarily to carry out the repair of churns.
Les Guard, later joined the Rural District Council's plumbing group before starting his own business.
Ivan Ridley, later played rugby for Petersfield and in his first years would cycle to work from Blackmore regularly.
David Lambert, didn't stay long. No comment!

Material suppliers to the business were for many years Gammon & Smith initially in Penns Road, but later in Swan Street before their final location to Bedford Road.

Their longest serving employee who saw three generations of the Hann family was Dick Heighes who joined the company in 1919 and remained until his retirement. Some record!

Other suppliers were, W P Winters, Portsmouth and The Metal Agencies, Bristol from whom the majority of materials were obtained in the 1950's and the 1960's as the company expanded. G A Day, Portsmouth, David Cover, Chichester and Reeves, Emsworth also supplied equipment.

Major works carried out during the 1960's included the installation of boiler plant and the heating, hot and cold water services to bungalows in the Readen House complex in Ramshill, new heating and hot water boilers in the Town Hall and the new heating boiler for the Methodist Church. These works showed a growth in the capabilities of the company to move into larger domains.

During the late 1960's I had decided to leave the business and concentrate on larger size heating installations. On the last day of 1969 I left Petersfield and moved to Sussex joining Thermal Contracts Limited at Haywards Heath. This was not very well accepted by my family although in later years I provided a considerable amount of consultancy to the company.

Harry jnr. and my brother Jeff decided to continue their plumbing and heating work as a partnership becoming H R Hann & Son. The business of H A Hann & Son was no more. From Harry snr's struggling days through to the expansion period of the 1960's the name had been part of Petersfield and very much a part of the whole Hann family, but now it is history. No 36 College Street had been sold during the late 1960's to the Wadham Stringer garage group and has now largely disappeared under housing. Finally my brother Jeff decided that the time was right to move on and dissolved the partnership in 1989 moving to Gloucestershire. Harry jnr. at the age of seventy retired.

A personal thought is that the company should have survived into the twenty first century with myself and Jeff at the helm with sensible expansion and an operating area much enlarged. Harry jnr. however remained tightly in control and although he gave lip service to a company with three family members in control this never came about hence two of us departing. So often this happens with family run businesses. Good people and good staff are lost and the families upset, the aftermath of this continuing for many years.

At 2012 Jeff is working alone as a plumber in Fareham and I have retired to Kent having spent a total of thirty six years in the building services industry and ten years in the bus and coach industry.

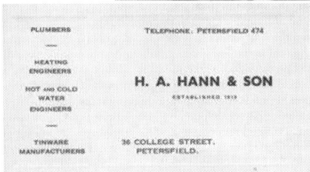

Early pictures of the front of the workshop at 36 College Street, Petersfield.
Complete with milk churns and the initial mode of transport. The top pictures
show the two Harrys` together with John Lancaster whilst the lower picture
includes Harry snr. And Mr Albuey.

The business card remained unaltered for many years

The H A Hann & Son stand at one of the Petersfield Trades Exhibitions in the Town Hall, Petersfield during the period that Harry jnr. was a member of the Petersfield Chamber Of Commerce.

The smaller boilers are of a size suitable for the normal two / three bedroom domestic property whereas the two larger boilers at the rear are for much larger houses aimed at the markets of the Durford Wood areas etc. All are solid fuel burning as oil fired and gas fired boilers had yet to be advanced enough for domestic use.

In the centre rear is one of the tiled fireplace surrounds of which many were installed in the Petersfield area by the company during its existence.

The annual exhibition became an excellent marketing tool for
H A Hann & Son

My brother Jeff doing the job he liked most. The photograph shows a large size domestic boiler which Jeff is in the process of installing in the Petersfield area.

The installation of a tidy well laid out pipework installation all fully labelled can be appreciated.

Vehicles owned by members of the family or by H A Hann & Son.

Top Left. Parked outside the new garage constructed in the garden of 36 College street are my own Ford Anglia car in highly polished dark blue finish, BTP236B, the first of the Ford Anglia vans painted dark green with gold nameboard, 237FAA, The second Ford Anglia van also in dark green, 874COT and Harry jnr`s Ford Cortina 1500 in blue and white, 312 LHO.

Top Right. Harry jnr`s Ford Zephyr Mk1 in green and cream, SKO 354.

Bottom. The Hillman Minx Estate purchased second hand in a dull grey after the repainting by Harry jnr. in a much lighter shade of grey.

The Zephyr and Minx are parked in Wadhams Yard which was next door to 36 College Street where for many years a large garage was rented.

THE HANN FAMILY TODAY

The story of my two families is almost complete. For my grandchildren they will now have some insite to their English history.

To any member of either family or to friends who may read this book I hope that I have been able to bring back a few memories of those who have now left us.

The final pages show my own immediate family at various times up until recently together with some additional information about the Hann family found whilst reading through the masses of records online.

Three people who I should mention, firstly my wife Sue for her support and encouragement and secondly my good friends Jeanette and Stephen Braybrook-Tucker for reading through the manuscript and checking the grammar etc.

The Hann Family

Additional Information Found Whilst Producing The Family Tree

1. James Hann, my great, great, great, grandfather was a Carrier in Beaminster, Dorset. The Carrier was the forerunner of many a country bus service in the early part of the twentieth century taking both people and goods from country to town and reverse.

2. George Fredric Hann left Yeovil for Wandsworth, London where he changed his surname from Hann to Hanne living at Islington, Brixton, Lambeth and Stratford before his death at Sanderstead, Surrey in 1928.

3. Thomas Herbert Hann had by 1867 moved to Hastings and had also changed his surname to Hanne. He later moved to Lee, London then to Battersea where he died in 1901.

4. William Cornelius Hann left Bournemouth for Tetbury, Gloucestershire then moved to Marylebone where he died in 1905.

5. By 1901 Charles Albert Hann had left Yeovil for Bristol.

6. Herbert Curtis Lee moved from Yeovil to Battersea having adopted the surname Hanne. Two years later he married his aunt Henriette Bernice Hann. *The surname spelling of Hanne is the prime link, but also is there a link with item 3?*

James and Lee with Sue and a bearded, hairy me at my parents home 22
Barham Road, Petersfield around 1975. The white painted build next door was
at one time the home of Sue`s parents Win and Bill Hall-Hadland with Sue
joining them for a short time before we married. My parents purchased No 22
sometime after Bill`s early death and Win moving back to the Brighton area.

The Barham Road houses gained considerable value and interest when the town
car park was constructed in wasteland between the houses and the town centre.
In many cases access was obtained to the properties at the rear directly from the
car park allowing many garages to be added in the rear gardens. From simple
Victorian / Edwardian terraced houses they became desirable town houses.

Children James and Lee with Sue and myself together with Sofia at my 60th birthday celebration at The Old Stables in Sheffield Park Gardens in Sussex. Sue had previously worked at the gardens as Visitor Services Manager for the National Trust.

My son James with his partner Julie at Sofia and Miguel`s christening
celebration in Coruche, Portugal.

Myself with granddaughter Sofia in one of our "mad" photo shots.

Some may well question, "what are they up to now?"

Photographed in the front garden of Paulo`s parents house in Sao Torcato near
Coruche in Portugal on the day of Sofia and Miguel`s christening in 2007.

My book is dedicated to Sofia and Miguel so that they will be aware
of their English heritage.